Family Quiz Tin

- For the first time, a quiz book for the whole family!
  - Quizzes covering all topics and age-graded so everyone can join in the fun.
  - Questions handpicked to ensure a level playing field.
- Your 8-year-old daughter is just as likely to win Quiz Time as her 82-year-old Granny.
  - The quizzes cover general knowledge & subject themes and are split into three age categories: Ages 12 and Under, Ages 13-18 and Ages 19+.
- Get your brains into gear and get ready for a night of truly competitive fun!
  - Play as individuals or in age group teams

GOOD LUCK

CONTENTS

GENERAL KNOWLEDGE 1

AGES 12 AND UNDER

1. What sort of creature is a dingo?

2. In which country would you find the Taj Mahal?

3. Who was the first man to walk on the moon?

4. What are the names of Harry Potter's parents?

5. Name two of the world's four oceans.

6. Which language is most often heard in Australia?

7. What is the name of the tree that produces acorns?

8. What is a baby kangaroo called?

9. How many sides does a hexagon have?

10. How many strings does a violin have?

Answers: *1. A wild dog. 2. India. 3. Neil Armstrong. 4. James and Lily. 5. Arctic, Atlantic, Indian and Pacific. 6. English. 7. Oak. 8. Joey. 9. Six. 10. Four.*

General Knowledge 1

AGES 13-18

1. What is the highest mountain in Great Britain?

2. What is the capital of New Zealand?

3. Which fairy tale character slept for a hundred years?

4. The Great Barrier Reef is located in which country?

5. In the nursery rhyme, who 'kissed the girls and made them cry'?

6. What sort of animal is the video game character Sonic?

7. In which forest do Robin Hood and his Merry Men live?

8. Helsinki is the capital city of which country?

9. How many pockets does a snooker table have?

10. On which continent is India located?

Answers: *1. Ben Nevis. 2. Wellington. 3. Sleeping Beauty. 4. Australia. 5. Georgie Porgie. 6. Hedgehog. 7. Sherwood. 8. Finland. 9. Six. 10. Asia.*

General Knowledge 1

AGES 19+

1. In what part of the body would you find the fibula?

2. Who wrote the acclaimed musical Hamilton?

3. How many of Henry VIII's wives were called Catherine?

4. Who is the main character in Catcher in the Rye?

5. Of which iconic 60s band was Ray Davies the front man?

6. Which popular video game has subtitles Modern Warfare and Black Ops?

7. In what US State is the city Nashville?

8. Which country was meant to host the cancelled 2020 Eurovision Song Contest?

9. What is seven cubed?

10. Who wrote the novels *Gone Girl* and *Sharp Objects*?

Answers: *1. The Leg. 2. Lin-Manuel Miranda. 3. Three. 4. Holden Caulfield. 5. The Kinks. 6. Call of Duty. 7. Tennessee. 8. The Netherlands. 9. 343. 10. Gillian Flynn.*

GENERAL KNOWLEDGE 2

AGES 12 AND UNDER

1. What is the name given to an animal that only eats plants?

2. In which year did the Second World War end?

3. What is Dr Who's time machine called?

4. What is the name of the organ that pumps blood around the body?

5. What two colours make up the flag of Spain?

6. How many hours are there in two days?

7. In "The Jungle Book", what kind of animal is Baloo?

8. What is the name of the tree that produces conkers?

9. What kind of food is pawpaw?

10. What is a baby goat called?

Answers: *1. A Herbivore. 2. 1945. 3. TARDIS. 4. The Heart. 5. Red and Yellow. 6. Forty-eight. 7. A Bear. 8. Horse Chestnut. 9. A Fruit. 10. A Kid.*

General Knowledge 2

AGES 13-18

1. How many years are there in a millennium?

2. What is the name of Harry Potter's pet owl?

3. What is the largest planet in the solar system?

4. What is the name of the mammoth in the Ice Age films?

5. Which artist painted the Mona Lisa?

6. What is the official residence of the President of the United States?

7. How many days are there in June?

8. What is the name of the Snowman in the film 'Frozen'?

9. What colour is the centre of the target in archery?

10. What is a female swan called?

Answers: *1. One thousand. 2. Hedwig. 3. Jupiter. 4. Manny. 5. Leonardo Da Vinci. 6. The White House. 7. Thirty. 8. Olaf. 9. Gold. 10. A Pen.*

General Knowledge 2

AGES 19+

1. Where in the world would you expect to find a car with the vehicle registration code 'V'?

2. In which children's book did a spider called Charlotte and a pig called Wilbur appear?

3. Which Mexican artist produced works entitled 'The Broken Column' and 'Diego and I'?

4. How many sides has a heptadecagon?

5. What was the name of the character played by John Travolta in the film 'Pulp Fiction'?

6. Which was the first James Bond film to feature Roger Moore in the title role?

7. 'Suncrisp', 'Golden Russet' and 'Braeburn' are all varieties of which fruit?

8. In which country would you find the coastal resort of Lara Beach?

9. In which year (within 10) was the first 'Grand National' horse race?

10. Rearrange the letters of the word 'allergy' to form three other seven-letter words.

Answers: 1. Vatican City. 2. Charlotte's Web. 3. Frida Kahlo. 4. Seventeen. 5. Vincent Vega. 6. Live and Let Die. 7. Apple. 8. Turkey. 9. 1839. 10. Gallery, Largely and Regally.

GENERAL KNOWLEDGE 3

AGES 12 AND UNDER

1. In which sport was Muhammad Ali a world champion?

2. What is the name of the lion in 'The Lion, The Witch and the Wardrobe'?

3. In which country is the Sphinx located?

4. Which chess piece can only move diagonally?

5. What colour belt are martial arts experts entitled to wear?

6. In the film 'Stuart Little', what kind of animal is Stuart?

7. What kind of creature is a Komodo dragon?

8. What name is given to someone who studies the stars?

9. What is the name of the invisible line that runs around the middle of the Earth?

10. Which word can go before ache, brush and paste to make three other words?

Answers: *1. Boxing. 2. Aslan. 3. Egypt. 4. The Bishop. 5. Black. 6. A Mouse. 7. A Lizard. 8. An Astronomer. 9. The Equator. 10. Tooth.*

General Knowledge 3

AGES 13-18

1. What instrument does a doctor use to learn if a person has a fever?

2. What does a botanist study?

3. What is the person who carriers a golfer's bag of clubs called?

4. In the movie 'The Lion King', what kind of animal is Timon?

5. What is the third planet from the sun?

6. Which of the seven dwarfs was beardless?

7. In which country did Joan of Arc lead an army?

8. What does a carnivore eat?

9. Which ocean is frozen for most of the year?

10. What is the centre of a hurricane called?

Answers: *1. A Thermometer. 2. Plants. 3. A Caddie. 4. A Meerkat. 5. Earth. 6. Dopey. 7. France. 8. Meat. 9. The Arctic. 10. The Eye.*

General Knowledge 3

AGES 19+

1. Who played the title character in the BBC series 'Jonathan Creek'?

2. Who succeeded Henry II as King of England?

3. John Gosden and Mark Johnston are prominent names in which sport?

4. Which app's logo consists of a telephone in a white speech bubble on a green background?

5. What was Baroness Thatcher's middle name?

6. What is the name of the fourth book in the 'Harry Potter' series?

7. Which is the first book of the Bible alphabetically?

8. What is fifteen percent of two thousand?

9. Which film actor has commonly been nicknames 'The Muscles from Brussels'?

10. How many episodes of the UK version of 'The Office' were made?

Answers: *1. Alan Davies. 2. Richard I/Richard the Lionheart. 3. Horse Racing. 4. WhatsApp. 5. Hilda. 6. Harry Potter and the Goblet of Fire. 7. Acts (sometimes referred to as The Acts so you can also accept Amos). 8. Three Hundred. 9. Jean-Claude Van Damme. 10. 14 (Two series of six episodes each, plus two longer Christmas Episodes).*

GENERAL KNOWLEDGE 4

AGES 12 AND UNDER

1. What colour are sapphires?

2. What is the coloured part of the eye that surrounds the pupil?

3. In which country are the Pyramids of Giza?

4. How many teeth should an adult have including their wisdom teeth?

5. What are the three primary colours?

6. What are the two longest rivers in the world?

7. Of which country is Brussels the capital?

8. What is a group of kangaroos called?

9. Which famous building did Guy Fawkes try to blow up?

10. What is the smallest ocean in the world?

Answers: *1. Blue. 2. The Iris. 3. Egypt. 4. Thirty-two. 5. Blue, Red and Yellow. 6. The Amazon and The Nile. 7. Belgium. 8. A Mob. 9. The Houses of Parliament. 10. The Arctic.*

General Knowledge 4

AGES 13-18

1. What magical item does Aladdin use to fly upon?

2. Of which African country was Nelson Mandela president?

3. What are the colours of the five Olympic rings?

4. What do tadpoles turn into?

5. Which is the largest ocean in the world?

6. In which Australian city is the famous Opera House?

7. What is the name of the plumber who features in several video games?

8. What is the largest country in Scandinavia?

9. What is the name of Peter Pan's pirate enemy?

10. Which planet is closest to the sun?

Answers: *1. A Carpet.   2. South Africa.   3. Blue, Black, Green, Red and Yellow.   4. Frogs. 5. The Pacific. 6. Sydney. 7. Mario. 8. Sweden. 9. Captain Hook. 10. Mercury.*

General Knowledge 4

AGES 19+

1. Who was the shortest-serving UK Prime Minister of the 20th century?

2. Which is the only letter in Scrabble to have a value of five points?

3. After which Dutch explorer was the island state of Tasmania named?

4. What is the product of the number of cards in a deck and the number of minutes in an hour?

5. Tobermory is on which Scottish island?

6. Which London Underground line has the most stations?

7. 'Hand on Your Heart', 'Wouldn't Change a Thing' and 'Tears on My Pillow' were all tracks on which 1990 studio album by Kylie Minogue?

8. Who wrote the books on which the series 'Game of Thrones' is based?

9. What is the national currency of Trinidad and Tobago?

10. How many football matches were played in total in the 2018 FIFA World Cup in Russia?

Answers: *1. Andrew Bonar Law. 2. K. 3. Abel Tasman. 4. Three thousand, one hundred and twenty. 5. Mull. 6. The District Line. 7. Enjoy Yourself. 8. George R. R. Martin. 9. The Trinidad and Tobago Dollar 10. Sixty-four.*

GENERAL KNOWLEDGE 5

AGES 12 AND UNDER

1. On which continent is the South Pole?

2. On which continent is the country of Brazil?

3. What word is used in tennis for the score of 40-40?

4. Can an ostrich fly?

5. What is the fiery liquid that flows from a volcano?

6. In the nursery rhyme who lost her sheep?

7. What is the name of the nanny played by Emma Thompson on film?

8. How many planets are there in the Solar System?

9. What type of animal is Bullseye in the "Toy Story" films?

10. What colour is a giraffe's tongue?

Answers: *1. Antarctica. 2. South America. 3. Deuce. 4. No. 5. Lava. 6. Bo Peep. 7. Nanny McPhee. 8. Eight. 9. A Horse. 10. Blue.*

General Knowledge 5

AGES 13-18

1. Which planet has a ring of rocks and ice?

2. What is a baby seal called?

3. What is the name of the main fairy in 'Peter Pan'?

4. In 'Finding Nemo', what is Nemo's dad called?

5. What is the name of the hero in 'The Lion King'?

6. What type of animal is a Labrador?

7. Buenos Aires is the capital city of which country?

8. What type of bird is a pintail?

9. What is the longest snake in the world?

10. In which sport do you 'catch a crab'?

Answers: *1. Saturn. 2. A Pup. 3. Tinkerbell. 4. Marlin. 5. Simba. 6. A Dog. 7. Argentina. 8. A Duck. 9. A Python. 10. Rowing.*

General Knowledge 5

AGES 19+

1. Which actor portrayed Samuel Johnson, writer of the first dictionary, in Blackadder the Third?

2. What are the three given names of Prince George of Cambridge?

3. Which English author created the priest-detective 'Father Brown'?

4. "Man, it's a hot one, like seven inches from the midday sun" - these are the opening lyrics of which 1999 hit?

5. BHD is the IATA code for which UK airport?

6. Who stood in as host on the first episode of 'Have I Got News For You' following Angus Deayton's departure in 2002?

7. How much is the purchase price of Old Kent Road in the London version of Monopoly?

8. Who is the alter ego of Sir Percy Blakeney?

9. Who was the sixth wife of Henry VIII?

10. In which century was William Shakespeare born?

Answers: 1. Robbie Coltrane. 2. George Alexander Louis. 3. G. K. Chesterton. 4. 'Smooth' by Santana. 5. George Best Belfast City Airport (accept Belfast). 6. Paul Merton. 7. £60. 8. The Scarlet Pimpernel. 9. Katharine Parr. 10. 16th Century (1564).

GENERAL KNOWLEDGE 6

AGES 12 AND UNDER

1. How many zeros are there in the number one thousand?

2. Who is Anna's sister in the Disney film 'Frozen'?

3. What is a young sheep called?

4. How many weeks are in a year?

5. In what country is the Great Barrier Reef?

6. What is half of the number fifty?

7. What is the biggest ocean on Earth?

8. When Humpty Dumpty was sitting on a wall, what happened next?

9. In Peppa Pig, what is Peppa's little brother called?

10. Which one of these is a fish: A shark, a whale or a dolphin?

Answers: *1. Three. 2. Elsa. 3. A Lamb. 4. Fifty-two. 5. Australia. 6. Twenty-five. 7. The Pacific. 8. He Had a Great Fall. 9. George. 10. A Shark.*

General Knowledge 6

AGES 13-18

1. Botany is the study of what?

2. What is the 10th letter of the alphabet?

3. There are three countries beginning with the letter 'F', can you name them?

4. Which scientist is known for inventing Penicillin?

5. What colour was the world's first adhesive postage stamp?

6. What hard white material are elephants' tusks made out of?

7. In which century was most of the Victorian era?

8. Which wizarding sport, which uses broomsticks, does Harry Potter play?

9. What was the first name of the artist who painted the 'Mona Lisa'?

10. Can you name the largest sandy desert in the world?

Answers: *1. Plants. 2. The Letter J. 3. France, Finland and Fiji. 4. Alexander Fleming. 5. Black. 6. Ivory. 7. 19th Century. 8. Quidditch. 9. Leonardo. 10. The Sahara.*

General Knowledge 6

AGES 19+

1. The Velocipede was a nineteenth-century prototype of what?

2. Which is Britain's oldest Sunday newspaper, published for the first time in 1791?

3. What was the middle name of Wolfgang Mozart?

4. What is the art of stuffing animals for preservation?

5. The term bhp is used when describing the power of a motor vehicle; for what does it stand?

6. What is Prince William's second name?

7. Who invented the Flying Shuttle in 1733?

8. What does a Geiger Counter measure?

9. If you are an LLD, what profession are you involved in?

10. Two of Henry VIII's wives were called Anne. Name them.

Answers: *1. The Bicycle. 2. The Observer. 3. Amadeus. 4. Taxidermy. 5. Brake Horse Power. 6. Arthur. 7. John Kay. 8. Radiation. 9. The Legal Profession. 10. Anne Boleyn and Anne of Cleves.*

GENERAL KNOWLEDGE 7

AGES 12 AND UNDER

1. How many colours are there in a rainbow?

2. Which animal is known as the 'Ship of the Desert?'

3. How many consonants are there in the English alphabet?

4. Which month of the year has the least number of days?

5. What do you call a house made of ice?

6. Which is the largest animal in the world?

7. Which is the tallest animal on the earth?

8. Which festival is known as the festival of colours?

9. Which festival is called the festival of light?

10. What type of bird lays the largest eggs?

Answers: *1. Seven. 2. The Camel. 3. Twenty-one. 4. February. 5. An Igloo. 6. The Blue Whale. 7. The Giraffe. 8. Holi. 9. Diwali. 10. The Ostrich.*

General Knowledge 7

AGES 13-18

1. Which is the largest country in the world?

2. Who invented the Computer?

3. How many players are there in a cricket team?

4. Which day is observed as World Literacy Day?

5. Who is the inventor of the radio?

6. Which place is known as the roof of the world?

7. How many teeth does a healthy adult have including the wisdom teeth?

8. Which gas is most abundant in the earth's atmosphere?

9. How many people are there in the world (to the nearest billion)?

10. Which is the continent with the most number of countries?

Answers: *1. Russia (by area). 2. Charles Babbage. 3. Eleven. 4. September 8th. 5. Marconi. 6. Tibet. 7. Thirty-two. 8. Nitrogen. 9. Seven (billion). 10. Africa.*

General Knowledge 7

AGES 19+

1. Who held the post of US president at the time of the coronation of Queen Elizabeth II?

2. In which English county is Blenheim Palace?

3. How many cards are there in the original version of the board game Cluedo?

4. What is the name of the machine, commonly referred to as a 'lie detector', which measures reactions such as blood pressure, pulse and respiration of an individual in response to questions asked?

5. Which English scientist and atheist wrote the best-selling 2006 book, 'The God Delusion'?

6. What was the first name of the founder of the pharmaceutical business 'Beecham's'?

7. Which comes first: Mothers' Day in the UK or Mothers' Day in the USA?

8. A vehicle with the national registration code 'PK' would originate from which country?

9. Who is attributed with the famous quote, "Be the change that you wish to see in the world"?

10. How many hours are there in a leap year?

Answers: *1. Dwight D. Eisenhower. 2. Oxfordshire. 3. Twenty-one. 4. The Polygraph. 5. Richard Dawkins. 6. Thomas. 7. The UK. 8. Pakistan. 9. Gandhi. 10. Eight thousand, seven hundred and eighty-four (24 x 366).*

GENERAL KNOWLEDGE 8

AGES 12 AND UNDER

1. The sun sets in which direction?

2. Which is the largest mammal?

3. What type of gas do plants absorb?

4. Which girl is one of Harry Potter's best friends?

5. Where is the Polar Express going?

6. Name two of the new Seven Wonders of the World.

7. How many years are there in a Century?

8. Name two of the world's oceans.

9. Which is the smallest continent?

10. Which is the densest jungle in the world?

Answers: *1. The West. 2. The Blue Whale. 3. Carbon Dioxide. 4. Hermione Granger. 5. To The North Pole. 6. Christ the Redeemer Statue in Brazil, Chichen Itza, Machu Picchu in Peru, Petra, The Roman Colosseum, The Great Wall of China or the Taj Mahal. 7. One hundred. 8. Any two of the Pacific, the Arctic, the Atlantic, the Indian and the Southern Oceans. 9. Australia. 10. The Amazon Rainforest.*

General Knowledge 8

AGES 13-18

1. Which is the tallest mountain in the world?

2. Which is the world's largest plateau?

3. Name either of the two founders of Microsoft.

4. Who came up with the theory of relativity?

5. How many millimetres are there in a centimetre?

6. Which planet is known as the red planet?

7. Which bird lays the largest eggs?

8. Which is the hardest substance found on Earth?

9. Which is the most spoken language in the world?

10. What name is given for a shape with ten sides?

Answers: *1. Mount Everest. 2. The Tibetan Plateau. 3. Bill Gates and Paul Allen. 4. Albert Einstein. 5. Ten. 6. Mars. 7. The Ostrich. 8. Diamond. 9. Mandarin Chinese. 10. Decagon.*

General Knowledge 8

AGES 19+

1. Which American actor was born Margaret Mary Emily Anne Hyra?

2. Only one British Prime Minister has been assassinated. Who was it?

3. Andrea, Caroline, Sharon and Jim made up which band?

4. How many bones, to the nearest ten, are there in a shark's body?

5. Which beer markets itself as 'The King of Beers'?

6. Which countryside animal would the French refer to as 'un hérisson'?

7. In which country would you find Zavratnica Bay?

8. Which author created the character Paddington Bear?

9. In which sport could you win the Davis Cup?

10. Which artist painted 'Lobster Telephone' in 1936?

Answers: *1. Meg Ryan. 2. Spencer Perceval. 3. The Corrs. 4. None (a shark's skeleton is made up entirely of cartilage). 5. Budweiser. 6. A Hedgehog. 7. Croatia. 8. Michael Bond. 9. Tennis. 10. Salvador Dali.*

GENERAL KNOWLEDGE 9

AGES 12 AND UNDER

1. To which famous band did Cheryl Cole belong?

2. What colour do you get if you mix yellow and blue?

3. In which American city is the Statue of Liberty?

4. How would you say 'hello' in French?

5. In which year did World War 2 start?

6. Which is the largest country in the United Kingdom?

7. The Wise Old Elf is a character in what TV show?

8. How many strings does a violin have?

9. How many years in a decade?

10. How many days are there in January?

Answers: *1. Girls Aloud. 2. Green. 3. New York. 4. Bonjour. 5. 1939. 6. England. 7. Ben and Holly's Little Kingdom. 8. Four. 9. Ten. 10. Thirty-one.*

General Knowledge 9

AGES 13-18

1. Who was the Prime Minister of the United Kingdom before Boris Johnson?

2. The Booker Prize is awarded in which field of the Arts?

3. Can you name the two Houses of Parliament?

4. What is the largest ocean in the world?

5. Polytheism is the belief that there is more than one what?

6. What is a male swan called?

7. How many leaves does a shamrock have?

8. Where does the Chancellor of the Exchequer live?

9. What word represents G in the International Radio Alphabet?

10. How many days are there in November?

Answers: *1. Theresa May. 2. Literature. 3. The Commons and The Lords. 4. The Pacific Ocean. 5. A God or Deity. 6. A Cob. 7. Three. 8. 11 Downing Street. 9. Golf. 10. Thirty.*

General Knowledge 9

AGES 19+

1. How many golden stars feature on the flag of the European Union?

2. In which world city would you find Maracanã Stadium?

3. Which word can come after 'dream', 'steam' and 'life' to form other words?

4. How many times did Pete Sampras win the Wimbledon Men's Singles title?

5. 'I think I'm gonna be sad, I think it's today...' These are the opening lyrics to which 1965 hit?

6. Emerald is the traditional birthstone associated with which month of the year?

7. Of which US state is Harrisburg the capital?

8. In which 'James Bond' film did Daniel Craig first play the starring role?

9. Which author wrote the original 'Poldark' series of books?

10. How many miles long is the River Nile (to the nearest 100 miles)?

Answers: *1. Twelve. 2. Rio de Janeiro (Brazil). 3. Boat. 4. Seven. 5. A Ticket to Ride (The Beatles). 6. May. 7. Pennsylvania. 8. Casino Royale (2006). 9. Winston Graham. 10. Four thousand, two hundred and fifty-eight miles long.*

GENERAL KNOWLEDGE 10

AGES 12 AND UNDER

1. Where does the UK prime minister live?

2. Which travels faster, light or sound?

3. What's the name of the cowboy in Toy Story?

4. How many wives did Henry VIII have?

5. What is the name of the world's largest reef system?

6. What famous islands were extensively studied by Charles Darwin?

7. What is the name of the third Harry Potter book?

8. What does a philatelist collect?

9. Which city has the largest population on Earth?

10. How many sides does an octagon have?

Answers: *1. 10 Downing Street. 2. Light. 3. Woody. 4. Six. 5. The Great Barrier Reef. 6. The Galapagos Islands. 7. Harry Potter and the Prisoner of Azkaban. 8. Stamps. 9. Tokyo. 10. Eight.*

General Knowledge 10

AGES 13-18

1. What is the colour of Absinthe?

2. What does DC stand for in electrical terminology?

3. *1989* is an album by which singer?

4. What is the biggest island in the world?

5. What sport did Michael Jordan play?

6. Someone born on the 3rd of November would have what star sign?

7. What herb is the central ingredient of the sauce pesto?

8. In which year (within 10 years) did the Eiffel Tower open?

9. What is Lady Gaga's real first name?

10. How many days (within 30 days) is an elephant pregnant for before giving birth (in days)?

Answers: *1. Green. 2. Direct Current. 3. Taylor Swift. 4. Greenland. 5. Basketball. 6. Scorpio. 7. Basil. 8. 1889. 9. Stefani. 10. 640-660 days.*

General Knowledge 10

AGES 19+

1. What year did the Titanic sink?

2. What is the title of the first ever Carry On film made and released in 1958?

3. What is the name of the biggest technology company in South Korea?

4. Which singer fronted the 1970s' pop group Showaddywaddy?

5. Which metal was discovered by Hans Christian Oersted in 1825?

6. How many breaths does the human body take daily (to the nearest thousand)?

7. Who was Prime Minister of Great Britain from 1841 to 1846?

8. What is the chemical symbol for silver?

9. What is the world's smallest bird?

10. Who played 'Bodie' and 'Doyle' in The Professionals?

Answers: 1. 1912. 2. Carry On Sergeant. 3. Samsung. 4. Dave Bartram. 5. Aluminium. 6. Twenty Thousand. 7. Robert Peel. 8. Ag. 9. The (Bee) Hummingbird. 10. Lewis Collins and Martin Shaw.

GENERAL KNOWLEDGE 11

AGES 12 AND UNDER

1. In computing, what are JPEGs, GIFs and TIFs?

2. What colour are the cheapest properties in Monopoly?

3. A golden jubilee is celebrated after how many years?

4. Which came first, the Stone Age or the Bronze Age?

5. In which Scottish city would you find The Royal Mile?

6. The Koran is the holy book of which religion?

7. Which countries make up Benelux?

8. What does a florist sell?

9. A Stetson is a type of what?

10. What is missing from a Manx cat?

Answers: *1. Images. 2. Brown. 3. Fifty. 4. The Stone Age. 5. Edinburgh. 6. Islam. 7. Belgium, Netherlands and Luxembourg. 8. Flowers. 9. A Hat. 10. Its Tail.*

General Knowledge 11

AGES 13-18

1. Alec Guiness and Ewan McGregor have both played which film character?

2. Marshall Mathers III is the real name of which rapper?

3. What instrument is used to measure atmospheric pressure?

4. The Dalai Lama is the spiritual leader of which religion?

5. Guinevere was the wife of which legendary king?

6. Which family lives at 742 Evergreen Terrace?

7. Teriyaki is a style of cooking from which country?

8. In which year was the Great Fire of London?

9. What is the highest female singing voice?

10. What is the name of Postman Pat's cat?

Answers: *1. Obi Wan Kenobi. 2. Eminem. 3. A Barometer. 4. Buddhism. 5. King Arthur. 6. The Simpsons. 7. Japan. 8. 1666. 9. Soprano. 10. Jess.*

General Knowledge 11

AGES 19+

1. Valentina Tereshkova became the first woman to do what?

2. In Dad's Army, what was Captain Mainwaring's first name?

3. Which country singer was known as The Man in Black?

4. Which newspaper launched a Sunday edition in 2012?

5. Which English King abdicated in 1936?

6. WildWood was a best-selling album for whom?

7. Which US State is known as The Golden State?

8. How many maids were a-milking in the song The 12 Days of Christmas?

9. Which country has won the Eurovision Song Contest the most often?

10. What was Coldplay's debut album?

Answers: *1. Go into Space. 2. George. 3. Johnny Cash. 4. The Sun. 5. Edward VIII. 6. Paul Weller. 7. California. 8. Eight. 9. Ireland. 10. Parachutes.*

GENERAL KNOWLEDGE 12

AGES 12 AND UNDER

1. On what form of transport would you find a Plimsoll Line?

2. Caledonia was the name for which country in the United Kingdom?

3. A silver jubilee is celebrated after how many years?

4. In what year did the Battle of Hastings take place?

5. Who led the plot to blow up the Houses of Parliament in 1605?

6. Lupine describes something as having qualities like what animal?

7. Huey, Dewey and Louie are the nephews of which Disney character?

8. Who is the eldest of Queen Elizabeth II's children?

9. On which side of a ship is starboard?

10. What is measured in decibels?

Answers: *1. A Ship. 2. Scotland. 3. Twenty-five. 4. 1066. 5. Guy Fawkes. 6. A Wolf. 7. Donald Duck. 8. Prince Charles. 9. Right. 10. Noise.*

General Knowledge 12

AGES 13-18

1. On what date do Americans celebrate Independence Day?

2. Jimmy Choo is famous for designing what?

3. Teams from which two countries traditionally compete for The Ashes?

4. The town of Melton Mowbray is famous for what kind of food?

5. In what year was the Act of Union between England and Scotland signed?

6. Which naturalist sailed on a ship called The Beagle?

7. In Romeo and Juliet who were the enemies of the Capulets?

8. How many deadly sins are there?

9. The clarinet is a member of which musical family?

10. What helicopter shares its name with a warm dry wind that blows in the Rocky Mountains?

Answers: *1. July 4th. 2. Shoes. 3. England and Australia. 4. Pork Pies. 5. 1707. 6. Charles Darwin. 7. The Montagues. 8. Seven. 9. Woodwind. 10. A Chinook.*

General Knowledge 12

AGES 19+

1. The assassination of which person sparked the First World War?

2. Which river flows easterly into the North Sea at Tilbury?

3. The Maghreb is a region of which continent?

4. Holly Golightly enjoyed what at Tiffany's?

5. Anthony Benedetto is the real name of which singer?

6. What was the name of the cruise ship that ran aground off the Italian coast in January 2012?

7. What is the largest democracy in the world?

8. Caviar comes from the eggs of which fish?

9. Scurvy is caused by a deficiency of which vitamin?

10. Who created the fictional detective Inspector Kurt Wallander?

Answers: *1. Archduke Franz Ferdinand. 2. The Thames. 3. Africa. 4. Breakfast. 5. Tony Bennett. 6. Costa Concordia. 7. India. 8. The Sturgeon. 9. Vitamin C. 10. Henning Mankell.*

GENERAL KNOWLEDGE 13

AGES 12 AND UNDER

1. What are Autobots and Decepticons?

2. Canines, molars and incisors are types of what?

3. Active, dormant and extinct refer to which geographical feature?

4. What is the largest desert in the world?

5. A car registration sticker bearing the initial DK is from which country?

6. Which cartoon character's catchphrase was, 'Er, what's up Doc?'?

7. Where would you find the Sea of Tranquility?

8. Barn, horned and long-eared are types of what bird?

9. Balthazar and Caspar were two of the Three Wise Men. Who was the third?

10. What is the young of a kangaroo called?

Answers: *1. Transformers. 2. Teeth. 3. Volcano. 4. The Sahara. 5. Denmark. 6. Bugs Bunny. 7. On the Moon. 8. Owl. 9. Melchior. 10. A Joey.*

General Knowledge 13

AGES 13-18

1. The musical We Will Rock You is based on the music of which band?

2. In ballet, which word describes rapid spinning on the toe of one foot?

3. Hydrophobia is the fear of what?

4. Thor was the Norse God of what?

5. What sign of the zodiac is represented by fish?

6. What is the name of the person who keeps the accounts on a ship?

7. In which ocean would you find the Falkland Islands?

8. Sternum is another name for which bone?

9. Mossad is the Intelligence Service of which country?

10. What is the Oxford Committee for Famine Relief better known as?

Answers: *1. Queen. 2. Pirouette. 3. Water. 4. Thunder. 5. Pisces. 6. The Purser. 7. The Atlantic. 8. Breastbone. 9. Israel. 10. Oxfam.*

General Knowledge 13

AGES 19+

1. An email address ending in .ie is for people from which country?

2. Rossini wrote an opera about which Swiss hero?

3. What illness is nicknamed the kissing disease?

4. The wine-producing region of Rioja is in which country?

5. How many years did Rip Van Winkle sleep for?

6. What type of oranges are usually used to make marmalade?

7. Oscar Wilde wrote the Ballad of which Gaol?

8. In internet dating, what does GSOH stand for?

9. On a London Underground map, what colour is the District Line?

10. What type of dish is Gazpacho?

Answers: *1. Republic of Ireland (Eire). 2. William Tell. 3. Glandular Fever. 4. Spain. 5. Twenty. 6. Seville Oranges. 7. Reading. 8. Good Sense of Humour. 9. Green. 10. A (cold) Soup.*

GENERAL KNOWLEDGE 14

AGES 12 AND UNDER

1. Haggis is a dish associated with which country?

2. In darts, how many points do you get for hitting the bullseye?

3. Londinium was the Roman name for which city?

4. Chop Suey is a dish common in which cuisine?

5. Cirrus, nimbus and cumulus are types of what?

6. What name is given to a group of four musicians?

7. What word describes the point from the centre of a circle to the perimeter?

8. From what London Station does the Hogwarts Express leave from?

9. In the Bible, which prophet baptised Jesus?

10. What is the fastest land mammal?

Answers: *1. Scotland. 2. Fifty. 3. London. 4. Chinese. 5. Cloud. 6. A Quartet. 7. Radius.*
8. King's Cross. 9. John the Baptist. 10. The Cheetah.

General Knowledge 14

AGES 13-18

1. Which Norwegian was the first man to reach the South Pole?

2. The Battle of Britain was an aerial conflict in which war?

3. Java, Kenyan and Colombian are varieties of what drink?

4. Mistral, Sirocco and Etesian are types of what?

5. Murrayfield is the home ground of which international rugby team?

6. What is the smallest continent on Earth?

7. What is an MP who is not a minister or shadow minister called?

8. What is the only station on the London Underground with London in its name?

9. Who were Scooby Doo's two human female companions?

10. Voodoo originated from which Caribbean country?

Answers: *1. Roald Amundsen.   2. World War Two.   3. Coffee.   4. Wind.   5. Scotland.   6. Australia. 7. A Backbencher. 8. London Bridge. 9. Velma and Daphne. 10. Haiti.*

General Knowledge 14

AGES 19+

1. With what song did Abba win Eurovision?

2. Hypertension is another name for what?

3. Little Rock is the capital of which American State?

4. Who was the Roman God of wine?

5. How many red balls are on a snooker table at the start of a frame?

6. In the Muppet Show, what nationality was the chef?

7. The musical instruction allegro means to play in what manner?

8. What is the longest river solely in England?

9. In what decade is the Korean War?

10. Zucchini is another word for which vegetable?

Answers: 1. Waterloo. 2. High Blood Pressure. 3. Arkansas. 4. Bacchus. 5. Fifteen. 6. Swedish. 7. Quickly. 8. The Thames. 9. 1950s. 10. Courgette.

GENERAL KNOWLEDGE 15

AGES 12 AND UNDER

1. What is the most expensive square in Monopoly?

2. In which Olympic sport do teams have to move backwards to win?

3. What is the name for a courtyard in a castle?

4. The yen is the currency of which country?

5. The Tasman Sea lies between which two countries?

6. What is the only rock eaten by humans?

7. What is traditionally eaten on Shrove Thursday?

8. What is the only digit that has the same number of letters as its value?

9. How many bones are there in the human body (to the nearest twenty)?

10. Stretching 4,500 miles, what is the longest mountain range in the world?

Answers: *1. Mayfair. 2. Rowing. 3. A Bailey. 4. Japan. 5. Australia and New Zealand. 6. Salt. 7. Pancakes. 8. Four. 9. 206. 10. The Andes.*

General Knowledge 15

AGES 13-18

1. Which U.S. State is known as the Sunshine State?

2. The ampere is used to measure what?

3. Which English Monarch was known as The Virgin Queen?

4. Tortillas, tacos and fajitas are common in which country's cuisine?

5. Who wrote the play A Midsummer Night's Dream?

6. What is the name of the protective leather trousers worn by American cowboys?

7. Something cooked au beurre is cooked in which ingredient?

8. Cha is the Chinese word for which drink?

9. The Hawaiian Islands lie in which ocean?

10. Which river flows through Newcastle?

Answers: *1. Florida. 2. Electrical Current. 3. Elizabeth I. 4. Mexico. 5. William Shakespeare. 6. Chaps. 7. Butter. 8. Tea. 9. The Pacific. 10. The Tyne.*

General Knowledge 15

AGES 19+

1. Robert Alan Zimmerman is the real name of which musician?

2. Sea parrot is another name for which bird?

3. The Rio Grande river forms the boundary between Mexico and which U.S. State?

4. Hibernia was the Roman name for which country?

5. Which Russian author wrote Crime and Punishment and The Brothers Karamazov?

6. What was the currency of the Netherlands before it joined the euro?

7. Which country duo had a hit with Islands in the Stream?

8. Which archbishop was murdered in Canterbury Cathedral?

9. What were the names of the two gangs in West Side Story?

10. What is the name of the central family in the TV drama Downton Abbey?

Answers: *1. Bob Dylan. 2. Puffin. 3. Texas. 4. Ireland. 5. Dostoevsky. 6. Guilder. 7. Kenny Rogers and Dolly Parton. 8. Thomas À Becket. 9. The Jets and The Sharks. 10. Crawley.*

GENERAL KNOWLEDGE 16

AGES 12 AND UNDER

1. Timpani, bass and side are examples of what type of instrument?

2. What is the second book of the Old Testament?

3. The Roman city of Pompeii was destroyed after the eruption of which volcano?

4. Pollo is the Italian name for what food?

5. The prancing horse is the logo of which car manufacturer?

6. How many years are in a millennium?

7. The Bayeux Tapestry depicts which battle?

8. Which figure from Greek mythology died after flying too close to the sun?

9. Igneous, sedimentary and metamorphic are types of what?

10. Samuel Pepys and Anne Frank are noted writers of what style of book?

Answers: *1. Drum. 2. Exodus. 3. Vesuvius. 4. Chicken. 5. Ferrari. 6. One thousand. 7. The Battle of Hastings. 8. Icarus. 9. Rock. 10. Diaries.*

General Knowledge 16

Ages 13-18

1. What word describes someone who does not believe in God?

2. Dermatology is the medical study of what?

3. Sayonara means goodbye in which language?

4. Arachnophobia is a fear of what kind of animal?

5. Which Irish county is also the name of a five-line nonsense poem?

6. The Globe Theatre specialises in works by which playwright?

7. Who was the Roman God of love?

8. What is the highest rank in the British Army?

9. What is the currency of India?

10. The BBBC is a governing body for which sport?

Answers: *1. Atheist. 2. The Skin. 3. Japanese. 4. Spider. 5. Limerick. 6. Shakespeare. 7. Cupid. 8. Field Marshall. 9. The Rupee. 10. Boxing.*

General Knowledge 16

AGES 19+

1. Hosni Mubarak was the former President of which country?

2. Vine Street and Bow Street are two of the orange properties in Monopoly. What is the third?

3. Bourbon comes from which state in America?

4. Which 16th Century astrologer is famous for his prophecies?

5. What is the text of an opera called?

6. Blanche Du Bois is the central character in which Tennessee Williams' play?

7. What is a somnambulist?

8. Haymarket and Waverley are train stations in which British city?

9. Who founded the Boy Scout movement?

10. What major conflict began in June 1950?

Answers: *1. Egypt. 2. Marlborough Street. 3. Kentucky. 4. Nostradamus. 5. The Libretto. 6. A Streetcar Named Desire. 7. A Sleepwalker. 8. Edinburgh. 9. Robert Baden-Powell. 10. The Korean War.*

GENERAL KNOWLEDGE 17

AGES 12 AND UNDER

1. A trimester is a period of how many months?

2. What do the stars on the American flag represent?

3. A hectare is a unit that measures what?

4. What is the national sport of Japan?

5. How many minutes does a rugby union match last?

6. What American city is nicknamed the City of Angels?

7. What is the largest U.S. State by area?

8. Which car manufacturer's slogan is Vorsprung durch Technik?

9. The River Taff flows through which British Capital City?

10. Which actor played Harry in the Harry Potter films?

Answers: *1. Three. 2. The Fifty States. 3. Area. 4. Sumo (Wrestling). 5. Eighty. 6. Los Angeles. 7. Alaska. 8. Audi. 9. Cardiff. 10. Daniel Radcliffe.*

General Knowledge 17

AGES 13-18

1. What colour are the stars on the Australian flag?

2. What is the capital of Hawaii?

3. Augustus Gloop and Veruca Salt are characters in which Roald Dahl book?

4. Who were the first winners of the football World Cup?

5. Kappa is a letter in which alphabet?

6. What name is given to the world's largest penguins?

7. Amaretti biscuits are flavoured using what type of nut?

8. What herb is usually used with onion in Christmas stuffing?

9. In the folk tale from which town did the Pied Piper come?

10. What shape is the pasta farfalle?

Answers: *1. White. 2. Honolulu. 3. Willy Wonka and the Chocolate Factory. 4. Uruguay. 5. Greek. 6. Emperor Penguins. 7. Almond. 8. Sage. 9. Hamelin. 10. Butterfly.*

General Knowledge 17

AGES 19+

1. Which actor played TV gangster Tony Soprano?

2. The Boer War was fought in which country?

3. Who was the Director of the FBI from 1924 until 1972?

4. Whose first number one single was Into the Groove?

5. What is the first event in the decathlon?

6. Which singer had 13 hits simultaneously in the UK top 40 in July 2009?

7. What is the art of clipping hedges more commonly known as?

8. Cosmology is the study of what?

9. What does a lepidopterist collect?

10. Which alcoholic beverage literally means 'water of life'?

Answers: *1. James Gandolfini. 2. South Africa. 3. J. Edgar Hoover. 4. Madonna. 5. 100 Metres. 6. Michael Jackson. 7. Topiary. 8. The Universe. 9. Butterflies (and moths). 10. Whisky.*

GENERAL KNOWLEDGE 18

AGES 12 AND UNDER

1. What word describes an angle that is greater than 90 degrees but less than 180 degrees?

2. In which European country was the first motorway built?

3. Nina, Pinta and Santa Maria were the three ships on which explorer's 1492 voyage to America?

4. What do the letters POV stand for on a film shoot?

5. Which English football team is nicknamed The Canaries?

6. How often does golf's Ryder Cup take place?

7. How many humps does a dromedary camel have?

8. What musical instrument was invented by Adolphe Sax?

9. What type of sandwiches does Paddington Bear like?

10. What is the most common first name for a Pope?

Answers: *1. Obtuse. 2. Germany. 3. Christopher Columbus. 4. Point of View. 5. Norwich City. 6. Every two years. 7. One. 8. The Saxophone. 9. Marmalade. 10. John.*

General Knowledge 18

AGES 13-18

1. What famous American road runs from Chicago to Los Angeles?

2. Lord Nelson died during which battle?

3. What is the last book of the New Testament?

4. In which city is the headquarters of the United Nations Security Council?

5. What is the holy day in Islam?

6. In which American State is the Grand Canyon?

7. Wine is the fermented juice of which fruit?

8. What is the main ingredient in guacamole?

9. In Greek mythology, who was God of the Sea?

10. The Webb-Ellis Trophy is awarded to the winners of which sporting competition?

Answers: *1. Route 66. 2. Battle of Trafalgar. 3. Revelation. 4. New York. 5. Friday. 6. Arizona. 7. Grape. 8. Avocado. 9. Poseidon. 10. The Rugby World Cup.*

General Knowledge 18

AGES 19+

1. What was the name of the hurricane that devastated New Orleans in 2005?

2. Which comedian hosted the snooker-themed gameshow Big Break?

3. Detective drama Lewis is set in which English city?

4. A car with the registration initials GBZ is from which British Overseas Territory?

5. Which playwright briefly married Marilyn Monroe?

6. In which European city can you travel on a railway system called the DART?

7. Barack Obama was born in which American State?

8. Which Tudor galleon was sunk in 1545 before being raised from the Solent in 1982?

9. In the Old Testament, who was cast into the lion's den by Nebuchadnezzar?

10. What was the virus H1N1 more commonly known as?

Answers: 1. Katrina. 2. Jim Davidson. 3. Oxford. 4. Gibraltar. 5. Arthur Miller. 6. Dublin. 7. Hawaii. 8. The Mary Rose. 9. Daniel. 10. Swine Flu.

GENERAL KNOWLEDGE 19

AGES 12 AND UNDER

1. Who painted the Mona Lisa?

2. Which planet is closest to the sun?

3. Which Scottish loch is said to be home to a mysterious monster?

4. Which English king was nicknamed Lionheart?

5. Complete the title of this James Bond film: The Man with the Golden...?

6. What is the Muslim month of fasting called?

7. What colour is Thomas the Tank Engine?

8. What is the official residence of the President of the United States?

9. The RSPB is a charity that protects which type of animal?

10. How many tentacles does an octopus have?

Answers: *1. Leonardo da Vinci. 2. Mercury. 3. Loch Ness. 4. Richard I. 5. Gun. 6. Ramadan. 7. Blue. 8. The White House. 9. Birds. 10. Eight.*

General Knowledge 19

AGES 13-18

1. Who was the first man to walk on the moon?

2. In fashion, what do the initials DKNY stand for?

3. Venison is the meat of which animal?

4. Stoke-on-Trent is located in which English county?

5. Which American Civil Rights Leader made the 'I Have a Dream' speech?

6. What is the name of the family in the comedy series 'Outnumbered'?

7. Which actor had Scotland Forever tattooed on his arm?

8. Daniel Craig made his debut as James Bond in which film?

9. Who was the first human child born in the Bible?

10. The Titanic set sail from which port on its maiden voyage?

Answers: *1. Neil Armstrong. 2. Donna Karan New York. 3. Deer. 4. Staffordshire. 5. Martin Luther King. 6. Brockman. 7. Sean Connery. 8. Casino Royale. 9. Cain. 10. Southampton.*

General Knowledge 19

AGES 19+

1. What is the largest U.S. State by population?

2. Who was the last British sovereign to lead an army into battle?

3. Who was the first presenter of A Question of Sport?

4. Which four U.S. States have the prefix New?

5. Martin Luther King and Robert Kennedy were both assassinated in which year?

6. You'll Never Walk Alone is a song from which Rodgers and Hammerstein musical?

7. Former UN General Secretary Kofi Annan is from which country?

8. Which novelist wrote Chitty Chitty Bang Bang?

9. What railway runs between Moscow and Vladivostok?

10. Which member of Monty Python made a guest appearance on TV comedy 'Cheers'?

Answers: *1. California. 2. George II. 3. David Vine. 4. Hampshire, Jersey, Mexico and York. 5. 1968. 6. Carousel. 7. Ghana. 8. Ian Fleming. 9. Trans-Siberian. 10. John Cleese.*

GENERAL KNOWLEDGE 20

AGES 12 AND UNDER

1. What are astronauts called in Russia?

2. A burqa is worn by women of which religion?

3. Maris Piper and King Edward are varieties of which vegetable?

4. Which of the Channel Islands is the largest?

5. What was the first name of Queen Victoria's husband?

6. What is the kitchen on a ship called?

7. Cash machines are known as ATMs. What does ATM stand for?

8. What animal lives in a drey?

9. In Oliver Twist, who owned a dog called Bullseye?

10. What is the English equivalent of the Spanish name Enrique?

Answers: *1. Cosmonauts. 2. Islam. 3. Potato. 4. Jersey. 5. Albert. 6. The Galley. 7. Automated Teller Machine. 8. A Squirrel. 9. Bill Sikes. 10. Henry.*

General Knowledge 20

AGES 13-18

1. What 'planet' was downgraded to a dwarf planet in 2006?

2. A kimono is a traditional costume in which country?

3. Which part of Germany gives its name to a famous gateau?

4. The most westerly point of mainland Europe is found in which country?

5. Who did David Cameron succeed as British prime minister?

6. Which director's films include Psycho, The Birds and Marnie?

7. Who is James Bond's boss?

8. In the Bible, how many gospels are there?

9. In motoring, what do the initials MOT stand for?

10. What is a female fox called?

Answers: *1. Pluto. 2. Japan. 3. The Black Forest. 4. Portugal. 5. Gordon Brown. 6. Alfred Hitchcock. 7. M. 8. Four. 9. Ministry of Transport. 10. A Vixen.*

General Knowledge 20

AGES 19+

1. Who designed St. Paul's Cathedral in London?

2. What constellation is also known as The Hunter?

3. On a clothes care label, what does a circle inside a square mean?

4. The Urals are located in which country?

5. Which U.S. President resigned from office in 1974?

6. The Office was set in which Berkshire town?

7. The Damned United was a film based on the life of which football manager?

8. Who sang the theme to the James Bond film Thunderball?

9. What was Robbie Williams' first UK number one solo single?

10. What is the name of the U.S. President's official plane?

Answers: *1. Sir Christopher Wren. 2. Orion. 3. Suitable for Tumble Drying. 4. Russia. 5. Richard Nixon. 6. Slough. 7. Brian Clough. 8. Tom Jones. 9. Millennium. 10. Air Force One.*

GENERAL KNOWLEDGE 21

AGES 12 AND UNDER

1. The Great Barrier Reef is found off the coast of which country?

2. With which mammals are vampires associated?

3. What is one-third of a pound to the nearest penny?

4. What do we call a blood vessel that carries blood away from the heart?

5. How many vowels are in the word miniature?

6. Which European country uses a different alphabet to English?

7. What liquid is essential for life?

8. In which mountain rage would you find the Matterhorn?

9. What is the fewest number of coins that make up 25p?

10. What is the square root of 100?

Answers: *1. Australia. 2. Bats. 3. Thirty-three pence. 4. An artery. 5. Five. 6. Greece. 7. Water. 8. The Alps. 9. Two. 10. Ten.*

General Knowledge 21

AGES 13-18

1. What were the Puritans called who sailed to America in 1620 to found a new colony?

2. Which Shakespearean character ignored the warning to 'Beware the Ides of March'?

3. What do we call any shape that has three or more sides?

4. What was Elvis Presley's middle name?

5. What colour are copper sulphate crystals?

6. What do the letters OS stand for when referring to maps?

7. Add together 52, 47 and 8?

8. What is the silent letter in the word chorus?

9. Who was the first King to rule both England and Scotland?

10. What is England's highest mountain?

Answers: *1. The Pilgrim Fathers. 2. Julius Caesar. 3. A polygon. 4. Aaron. 5. Blue. 6. Ordnance Survey. 7. 107. 8. H. 9. James I. 10. Scafell Pike.*

General Knowledge 21

AGES 19+

1. In which county would you find Leeds Castle?

2. William Henry Pratt was the real name of which actor?

3. What is the name of the nightclub in the TV drama series, 'The Sopranos'?

4. Which composer wrote the opera Aida?

5. What is measured in joules?

6. The musical My Fair Lady was based on which play by George Bernard Shaw?

7. Who was the first presenter of 'A Question of Sport'?

8. What type of bread takes its name from the Italian word for slipper?

9. Which pop group, formed in the 70s, took their name from a British cinema chain?

10. What animal lives in den called a holt?

Answers: *1. Kent. 2. Boris Karloff. 3. Bada Bing. 4. Verdi. 5. Energy. 6. Pygmalion. 7. David Vine. 8. Ciabatta. 9. Roxy Music. 10. An otter.*

GENERAL KNOWLEDGE 22

AGES 12 AND UNDER

1. Calculate: 8 x 100 divided by 8?

2. What nationality was the footballer Diego Maradona?

3. What do we call the very hard substance on the outside of a tooth?

4. In Greek mythology, what kind of creature was Pegasus?

5. Which animal's tail is called a brush?

6. What is a pecan: a bird, a hat or a nut?

7. What do people do in the Royal Mint?

8. If you have amnesia, what have you lost?

9. Which wizard helped King Arthur?

10. What is the name of the bear in The Jungle Book?

Answers: *1. 100. 2. Argentinian. 3. Enamel. 4. A winged horse. 5. Fox. 6. A nut. 7. Make coins. 8. Your memory. 9. Merlin. 10. Baloo.*

General Knowledge 22

AGES 13-18

1. In which country would you find Ayers Rock?

2. What is the largest country in South America?

3. Which one of the Beatles was married to Yoko Ono?

4. In the Bible, how many apostles were there?

5. How many seconds are there in 20 minutes?

6. Who wrote Murder on the Orient Express?

7. How many holes are there on a standard golf course?

8. What kind of animal is a Rottweiler?

9. What do the letters RAF stand for?

10. The olfactory nerve is connected with which one of our senses?

Answers: *1. Australia. 2. Brazil. 3. John Lennon. 4. Twelve. 5. 1200. 6. Agatha Christie. 7. 18. 8. A dog. 9. Royal Air Force. 10. Smell.*

General Knowledge 22

AGES 19+

1. What nationality was the composer Berlioz?

2. What was the name of the housekeeper in Father Ted?

3. Which two US States start with the word North?

4. In what year was the Magna Carta signed?

5. Dave Hill was guitarist with which glam rock band?

6. Jesus of Nazareth was crucified on which mountain?

7. How many pairs of chromosomes are there in the human body?

8. Which novel by Charles Dickens is also known as The Parish Boy's Progress?

9. What is the only American State that is one syllable long?

10. In the cartoon the Wacky Races, who drove the Bouldermobile?

Answers: *1. French. 2. Mrs Doyle. 3. Carolina and Dakota. 4. 1215. 5. Slade. 6. Golgotha. 7. 23. 8. Oliver Twist. 9. Maine. 10. The Slag Brothers.*

GENERAL KNOWLEDGE 23

AGES 12 AND UNDER

1. Does a lion use its teeth or its claws to kill its prey?

2. Which of Roald Dahl's characters owned a chocolate factory?

3. What kind of animal is a cockatoo?

4. How many years does a bicentenary mark?

5. Which sport are the West Indies famous for?

6. In which European country would you find the cities of Salzburg and Innsbruck?

7. What are the three colours of the Italian flag?

8. What kind of animal is a Red Admiral?

9. Which is longer: 3 hours or 170 minutes?

10. What is the plural of leaf?

Answers: *1. Teeth. 2. Willy Wonka. 3. A bird. 4. Two hundred. 5. Cricket. 6. Austria. 7. Red, white and green. 8. A butterfly. 9. 3 hours. 10. Leaves.*

General Knowledge 23

AGES 13-18

1. What is the name given to a flag, which displays a skull and crossbones?

2. Which wall was the longest structure in the Roman Empire?

3. What is the world's highest mountain range?

4. What kind of dance music is Johann Strauss famous for?

5. What title was given to the emperors of Russia?

6. If two angles of a triangle are 35° and 65°, what is the third angle?

7. What is a male rabbit called?

8. What was Picasso's first name?

9. Hamlet was the Prince of which country, in the Shakespeare play of the same name?

10. What is a *mambo*?

Answers: *1. Jolly Roger. 2. Hadrian's Wall. 3. The Himalayas. 4. Waltz music. 5. Tsar. 6. 80°. 7. A buck. 8. Pablo. 9. Denmark. 10. A dance.*

General Knowledge 23

AGES 19+

1. Maggie and Brick are the central characters in which play by Tennessee Williams?

2. Who was the first man to fly solo across the Atlantic?

3. Springtime for Hitler is a song from which musical?

4. What was the scheduled destination of the Titanic on its ill-fated maiden journey?

5. The Magna Carta was signed by which King?

6. How long is the M25 motorway?

7. What was the name of the computer in Red Dwarf?

8. What character did Alan Rickman play in Die Hard?

9. In the name of the sports car manufacturer, what do the initials MG stand for?

10. What was the name of the policeman in Top Cat?

Answers: *1. Cat on a Hot Tin Roof. 2. Charles Lindbergh. 3. The Producers. 4. New York. 5. King John. 6. 117 miles (give a point for 5 miles either way). 7. Holly. 8. Hans Gruber. 9. Morris Garages. 10. Officer Dibble.*

GENERAL KNOWLEDGE 24

AGES 12 AND UNDER

1. With which part of the body is the auditory nerve associated?

2. What is 2.37 to the nearest whole number?

3. What kind of paper can detect acids and alkali?

4. How many years in a decade?

5. Which sport is played with sticks and a puck?

6. What is the opposite of narrow?

7. Is reggae a type of food, music or clothing?

8. Which is more: 4 litres or 6 pints?

9. Which country do Porsche cars come from?

10. How many consonants are in the word commitment?

Answers: *1. The ear. 2. Two. 3. Litmus paper. 4. Ten. 5. Ice hockey. 6. Wide. 7. Music. 8. Four litres. 9. Germany. 10. Seven.*

General Knowledge 24

AGES 13-18

1. What nationality was Josef Stalin?

2. Who wrote The Jungle Book?

3. In the Trojan War, who fought against the Trojans?

4. What is Europe's largest island?

5. What do we call a doctor who specialises in skin diseases?

6. If you travelled from Liverpool to Dublin, which sea would you cross?

7. What is 5% of 120?

8. In the human body, what is the common name for the trachea?

9. What kind of musical instrument is a Stradivarius?

10. In which American city is Hollywood?

Answers: *1. Russian. 2. Rudyard Kipling. 3. The Greeks. 4. Great Britain. 5. A dermatologist. 6. The Irish Sea. 7. Six. 8. The windpipe. 9. A violin. 10. Los Angeles.*

General Knowledge 24

AGES 19+

1. In what year was the wearing of seatbelts in cars made compulsory in Britain?

2. What was the name of author Ian Fleming's Jamaican home?

3. With what song did Katrina and the Waves win the Eurovision Song Contest?

4. What was the name of Lord Nelson's flagship at the Battle of Trafalgar?

5. Who founded The Body Shop?

6. The Scotsman newspaper is published in which city?

7. Which two US States don't have a border with any other State?

8. Played by Hugh Laurie, what is the first name of Doctor House?

9. The abandoned Mayan city of Chichen Itza lies in which modern-day country?

10. On what day of the week were The Cure in love?

Answers: 1. 1983 (give a point for an answer one year either way). 2. Goldeneye. 3. Love Shine a Light. 4. HMS Victory. 5. Anita Roddick. 6. Edinburgh. 7. Alaska and Hawaii. 8. Gregory. 9. Mexico. 10. Friday.

GENERAL KNOWLEDGE 25

AGES 12 AND UNDER

1. In which country is the airline Qantas based?

2. What is the opposite of innocent?

3. In which country is the Costa del Sol?

4. What colour of flag means 'surrender'?

5. What is the name of London's busiest airport?

6. What is the full name of the football club known as Spurs?

7. What is the official language of Mexico?

8. In the films, what was Rocky's profession?

9. What is the main religion of Pakistan?

10. How many British Kings named George have there been?

Answers: *1. Australia. 2. Guilty. 3. Spain. 4. White. 5. Heathrow. 6. Tottenham Hotspur. 7. Spanish. 8. Boxing. 9. Islam. 10. Six.*

General Knowledge 25

AGES 13-18

1. What name is given to the coloured part of the eye?

2. How many playing cards are there in a pack?

3. In which game might you hear the words 'Strike Three'?

4. Name China's largest city by population?

5. On which date do Americans celebrate Independence Day?

6. What surname was adopted by the British Royal Family in 1917?

7. What were the first Norman castles in England made of?

8. What is made when grape juice is fermented?

9. Which Scottish leader gained strength from watching a spider?

10. The song 'Climb Every Mountain' comes from which musical film?

Answers: *1. The iris. 2. 52. 3. Baseball. 4. Shanghai. 5. The Fourth of July. 6. Windsor. 7. Timber 8. Wine. 9. Robert the Bruce. 10. The Sound of Music.*

General Knowledge 25

AGES 19+

1. According to the nursery rhyme, which child has far to go?

2. What was the name of Dr Who's mechanical dog?

3. What is the oldest University in Britain?

4. Which former Miss Ohio won the Oscar for Best Actress in 2002?

5. What is the largest landlocked country in the world?

6. Which singer won the first series of Britain's Got Talent?

7. In what year was Prince Charles born?

8. What was the first TV Programme to appear on Channel 4?

9. Plantain is the cooking variety of which fruit?

10. The Golden Temple is in which Indian city?

Answers: *1. Thursday's. 2. K9. 3. Oxford. 4. Halle Berry. 5. Mongolia. 6. Paul Potts. 7. 1948. 8. Countdown. 9. Banana. 10. Amritsar.*

CAPITALS AND COUNTRIES

AGES 12 AND UNDER

1. Name the capital of England?

2. In which country would find the city of Paris?

3. What is the capital of Germany?

4. In which continent would you find Iceland?

5. What is the capital of Russia?

6. Spell PORTUGAL?

7. What is the capital of Portugal?

8. Name the capital of Scotland?

9. In which continent would you find the country of Morocco?

10. Stockholm is the capital of which country?

Answers: *1. London. 2. France. 3. Berlin. 4. Europe. 5. Moscow. 6. PORTUGAL. 7. Lisbon. 8. Edinburgh. 9. Africa. 10. Sweden.*

Capitals and Countries

AGES 13-18

1. Name the capital of the USA?

2. In which country would find the city of Copenhagen?

3. What is the capital of Greece?

4. In which continent would you find Vietnam?

5. What is the capital of India?

6. Spell JAMAICA?

7. What is the capital of the Netherlands?

8. Name the capital of Northern Ireland?

9. In which continent would you find the country of Malawi?

10. Belgrade is the capital of which country?

Answers: *1. Washington, D.C. 2. Denmark. 3. Athens. 4. Asia. 5. New Delhi. 6. JAMAICA. 7. Amsterdam. 8. Belfast. 9. Africa. 10. Serbia.*

Capitals and Countries

AGES 19+

1. Name the capital of Switzerland?

2. In which country would find the city of Minsk?

3. What is the capital of Finland?

4. In which continent would you find the Maldives?

5. What is the capital of Pakistan?

6. Spell LIECHTENSTEIN?

7. What is the capital of Croatia?

8. Name the capital of Wales?

9. In which continent would you find the country of Papua New Guinea?

10. Riga is the capital of which country?

Answers: *1. Bern. 2. Belarus. 3. Helsinki. 4. Asia. 5. Islamabad. 6. LIECHTENSTEIN. 7. Zagreb. 8. Cardiff. 9. Australasia (Oceania). 10. Latvia.*

CAPITALS CITIES

AGES 12 AND UNDER

Name the capital city of:

1. Italy.

2. United States.

3. Greece.

4. France.

5. Egypt.

6. Spain.

7. Japan.

8. England.

9. Thailand.

10. Russia.

Answers: 1. Rome. 2. Washington, DC. 3. Athens. 4. Paris. 5. Cairo. 6. Madrid. 7. Tokyo. 8. London. 9. Bangkok. 10. Moscow.

Capitals Cities

AGES 13-18

Name the capital city of:

1. Sweden.

2. Australia.

3. Wales.

4. Argentina.

5. Iraq.

6. South Korea.

7. Mexico.

8. Ireland.

9. Canada.

10. Brazil.

Answers: *1. Stockholm. 2. Canberra. 3. Cardiff. 4. Buenos Aires. 5. Baghdad. 6. Seoul. 7. Mexico City. 8. Dublin. 9. Ottawa. 10. Brasilia.*

Capitals Cities

AGES 19+

Name the capital city of:

1. Belgium.

2. Jamaica.

3. Venezuela.

4. Morocco.

5. Bangladesh.

6. Ukraine.

7. Kenya.

8. Austria.

9. Vietnam.

10. Fiji.

Answers: *1. Brussels. 2. Kingston. 3. Caracas. 4. Rabat. 5. Dhaka. 6. Kiev. 7. Nairobi. 8. Vienna. 9. Hanoi. 10. Suva.*

GEOGRAPHY

AGES 12 AND UNDER

1. In which American city is the Golden Gate Bridge located?

2. Madagascar is surrounded by which Ocean?

3. Mount Everest lies in which mountain range?

4. The United States of America consists of how many states?

5. Which country has the largest population in the world?

6. Which is the longest river in Africa?

7. Europe and Africa are separated by which sea?

8. Which Italian city is famed for its canals?

9. What is the hottest continent on Earth?

10. What is the nickname for New York City?

Answers: *1. San Francisco. 2. The Indian Ocean. 3. The Himalayas. 4. 50. 5. China. 6. The Nile. 7. The Mediterranean. 8. Venice. 9. Africa. 10. The Big Apple.*

Geography

Ages 13-18

1. Which country calls itself Nippon?

2. Which large river flows through London?

3. What natural wonder is named after aviator Jimmy Angel?

4. Which Scottish loch has a length of 24 miles?

5. Which island country lies off China, Korea and Russia?

6. Which two countries share the longest border in the world?

7. Which country is the most populated in the European Union?

8. What is the line of latitude that runs around the centre of the world called?

9. Which country's name contains only four letters and ends in a q?

10. Which river flows through Glasgow?

Answers: *1. Japan. 2. The Thames. 3. Angel Falls. 4. Loch Ness. 5. Japan. 6. USA and Canada.*
7. Germany. 8. The Equator. 9. Iraq. 10. The Clyde.

Geography

AGES 19+

1. Which is the only bascule bridge in London, whose road can be raised from either side to allow ships

to pass through?

2. What river flows through the Grand Canyon?

3. What four countries surround the Czech Republic?

4. What is the only country through which the Equator and the Tropic of Capricorn pass?

5. What is the capital city of Slovenia, once part of the state of Yugoslavia?

6. Which country is nicknamed 'The Cockpit of Europe' because of the number of battles fought on its

soil?

7. Apart from Dutch and French, what is other official language of Belgium?

8. What was the name of the supercontinent of 200 million years ago?

9. Which country is called 'The Land of the Rising Sun'?

10. What is the largest of the Channel Islands?

Answers: *1. Tower Bridge. 2. The Colorado. 3. Germany, Poland, Slovakia and Austria (award a point for three correct answers). 4. Brazil. 5. Ljubljana. 6. Belgium. 7. German. 8. Pangaea. 9. Japan. 10. Jersey.*

HISTORY

AGES 12 AND UNDER

1. In which country was mummification carried out on important people when they died?

2. How many wives did Henry VIII have?

3. Which people travelled in long ships and raided Britain in early medieval times?

4. What title was given to rulers of Ancient Egypt?

5. What colour are the benches in the House of Commons?

6. Who was the 'Lady with the Lamp' during the Crimean War?

7. With which Queen is the phrase 'We are not amused' associated?

8. What famous structure was erected on Salisbury Plane in the third millennium B.C.?

9. Air Force One is a plane used by the holder of what position?

10. Who took elephants across the Alps?

Answers: *1. Egypt. 2. Six. 3. The Vikings. 4. Pharaoh. 5. Green. 6. Florence Nightingale. 7. Queen Victoria. 8. Stonehenge. 9. The President of the United States of America. 10. Hannibal.*

History

AGES 13-18

1. In which year did World War 1 commence?

2. In which country was Adolf Hitler born?

3. In which American city was John F. Kennedy assassinated?

4. The Magna Carta was published by the King of which country?

5. Which Roman Emperor built a wall across the northernmost point of Roman Britannia in 122 A.D.?

6. Which London theatre is associated with William Shakespeare?

7. The Khmer Rouge was a regime that ruled which nation during the 20th Century?

8. Marco Polo was the first European explorer to reach which country?

9. In which decade did the USA become involved in the Korean War?

10. What is celebrated in America on the 4th of July?

Answers: *1. 1914. 2. Austria. 3. Dallas. 4. England. 5. Hadrian. 6. The Globe. 7. Cambodia. 8. China. 9. 1950s. 10. Independence Day.*

History

AGES 19+

1. Which queen had the shortest reign of Henry VIII's six wives?

2. In which country would you find The Bay of Pigs?

3. Which medieval queen was married to both Louis VII of France and Henry II of England?

4. Who was the first human to journey into Space?

5. Julius Caesar was assassinated on the 15th of March, 44 B.C., a date that is known by what term?

6. Where did the Great Fire of London begin in September 1666?

7. Which king preceded Queen Victoria?

8. Who was the mother of Emperor Nero and the wife of Emperor Claudius?

9. Where was Napoleon Bonaparte born?

10. In which decade did the potato famine strike Ireland?

Answers: *1. Anne of Cleves. 2. Cuba. 3. Eleanor of Aquitaine. 4. Yuri Gagarin. 5. The Ides of March. 6. Pudding Lane (or Fish Yard). 7. William IV. 8. Agrippina (the Younger). 9. Corsica. 10. 1840s.*

MUSIC

AGES 12 AND UNDER

1. 'The Star-Spangled Banner' is the national anthem of which country?

2. Justin Bieber comes from which country?

3. Which large stringed instrument is also the national instrument of Wales?

4. Victoria Beckham and Emma Bunton used to be in which famous girl band?

5. Starting with the letter x, which musical instrument consists of wooden bars struck by a mallet?

6. 'Pure Imagination' is a song from which children's film?

7. Who won many awards for her song 'Hello'?

8. Which musical instrument is made up of a small hoop with metal discs inserted along its frame?

9. In the nursery song 'The Wheels on the Bus', what goes 'swish, swish, swish'?

10. In which movie do orphans sing the song 'Food, Glorious Food'?

Answers: *1. USA. 2. Canada. 3. The Harp. 4. The Spice Girls. 5. Xylophone. 6. Willy Wonka and the Chocolate Factory. 7. Adele. 8. Tambourine. 9. The Wipers. 10. Oliver.*

Music

AGES 13-18

1. Freddie Mercury was lead singer with which legendary pop group?

2. Is Beethoven famous for pop music, classical music or jazz?

3. In the young children's song, what exactly 'climbed up the waterspout'?

4. Which musical instrument did Louis Armstrong play?

5. 'The Bare Necessities' is a song from which animated 1967 Disney film?

6. What name is given to the group of musical instruments that make sounds by being struck?

7. Complete the title of the following song from the musical film 'Mary Poppins': 'A Spoonful of...'.

8. The ukulele looks like a small version of which instrument?

9. Name the musical instrument that is also a three-sided shape.

10. Jiminy Cricket sang 'When You Wish Upon a Star' in which Disney film?

Answers: *1. Queen. 2. Classical Music. 3. Itsy Bitsy Spider. 4. The Trumpet. 5. The Jungle Book. 6. Percussion. 7. Sugar. 8. The Guitar. 9. The Triangle. 10. Pinocchio.*

Music

AGES 19+

1. What is the name of Dua Lipa's 2020 album release?

2. Name the song and the artist for the following lyric: 'Maybe I'm foolish, maybe I'm blind, thinking I

can see through this and see what's behind'?

3. Matt Goss, Luke Goss and Craig Logan made up which band?

4. In what year did The Beatles split up?

5. What is rapper P Diddy's real name?

6. Complete this Spice Girls lyric: 'If you wanna be my [BLANK], you gotta get with my friends'?

7. Which two musicians collaborated on 'Another Way to Die', the theme song to the 2008 Bond movie,

'Quantum of Solace'?

8. Gary and Martin Kemp were in which band?

9. In what decade was pop icon Madonna born?

10. Which two country singers sang a duet on the 1983 song 'Islands in the Stream'?

Answers: *1. Future Nostalgia. 2. Human by Rag'n'Bone Man. 3. Bros. 4. 1970. 5. Sean Combs. 6. Lover. 7. Alicia Keys and Jack White. 8. Spandau Ballet. 9. 1950s (1958). 10. Kenny Rogers and Dolly Parton.*

FILM AND TV

AGES 12 AND UNDER

1. Which girl is one of Harry Potter's best friends?

2. In 'Beauty and the Beast', which wing of the castle is Belle forbidden to go to?

3. What is the name of the cowgirl in 'Toy Story'?

4. Mary Poppins is the nanny to which family?

5. In 'The Little Mermaid', what kind of animal is Sebastian?

6. What kind of animal is Aslan in 'The Chronicles of Narnia'?

7. Where is the Polar Express going?

8. When Nemo was put in a fish tank, what new name did the other fish give him?

9. What is the name of Peppa Pig's younger brother?

10. What is the name of the Cockapoo in 'Paw Patrol'?

Answers: *1. Hermione (Grainger). 2. The West Wing. 3. Jessie. 4. The Banks Family. 5. A (Red Jamaican) Crab. 6. A Lion. 7. The North Pole. 8. Sharkbait. 9. George. 10. Skye.*

Film and TV

Ages 13-18

1. What animal did Babe want to be?

2. Who was the only one of the seven dwarfs who did not have a beard?

3. In which Christmas movie does James Caan play the father of Will Ferrell?

4. In the 1999 movie 'A Bug's Life', what species were the bad guys?

5. What is the name of the king monkey in 'The Jungle Book'?

6. Who played Inspector Gadget in the 1999 live-action movie?

7. In which James Bond film did Sean Bean play 006?

8. Which Hollywood actress voices Princess Fiona in 'Shrek'?

9. In Disney's cartoon version of Robin Hood, what kind of animal was Robin Hood?

10. What kind of animal is Pepe, star of the Muppets' Wizard of Oz?

Answers: *1. A Sheep Dog. 2. Dopey. 3. Elf. 4. Grasshoppers. 5. Louie/Louis. 6. Matthew Broderick. 7. Goldeneye. 8. Cameron Diaz. 9. A Fox. 10. A King Prawn.*

Film and TV

AGES 19+

1. Which 1995 submarine drama feature uncredited additional dialogue courtesy of Quentin Tarantino?

2. What was the name of the 2019 sequel to Stanley Kubrick's 'The Shining'?

3. Who plays the titular role in the 2018 superhero film 'Black Panther'?

4. What planet are Transformers from?

5. Which Marilyn Monroe film featured the song 'Diamonds Are a Girl's Best Friend'?

6. Which Beyoncé hit does Liza Minnelli sing in 'Sex and the City 2'?

7. In what year did 'Coronation Street' first air on ITV?

8. What is the name of Tony's dog in 'After Life'?

9. What is the name of Quint's shark-hunting boat in 'Jaws'?

10. For which film did Sandra Bullock win her Oscar (as of 2020)?

Answers: *1. Crimson Tide. 2. Doctor Sleep. 3. Chadwick Boseman. 4. Cybertron. 5. Gentlemen Prefer Blondes. 6. Single Ladies. 7. 1960. 8. Brandy. 9. The Orca. 10. The Blind Side.*

LITERATURE

AGES 12 AND UNDER

1. Who wrote 'Romeo and Juliet'?

2. What is the name of the bank where Harry Potter deposits his wizard money?

3. Who wrote tales about Flopsy, Mopsy and Cottontail?

4. In which city did Anne Frank live when she wrote her famous diary?

5. Is the first book of the Bible, Exodus, Genesis or Psalms?

6. In the nursery rhyme, what did the cow jump over?

7. Which doctor is famous for 'Green Eggs and Ham' and other funny stories?

8. Which book featured a man-child called Mowgli?

9. What word means a book written by a person about their life?

10. Who had a teddy bear called Winnie the Pooh?

Answers: *1. William Shakespeare. 2. Gringott's. 3. Beatrix Potter. 4. Amsterdam. 5. Genesis. 6. The Moon. 7. Dr. Seuss. 8. The Jungle Book. 9. Autobiography. 10. Christopher Robin.*

Literature

Ages 13-18

1. Who wrote 'Animal Farm'?

2. In 'Tom's Midnight Garden', who was Tom's friend from another age?

3. Which town is closely associated with William Shakespeare?

4. Who is the world's most successful horror writer, whose books include 'Misery' and 'The Shining'?

5. What is the name of the dog in 'Peter Pan'?

6. Which famous author wrote 'Bleak House'?

7. Which children's book character had a friend called Big Ears?

8. About what kind of animal is the book 'Black Beauty'?

9. What kind of creature was Bilbo Baggins?

10. Which famous detective's first appearance was in the book 'The Mysterious Affair at Styles'?

Answers: *1. George Orwell.   2. Hattie.   3. Stratford-upon-Avon.   4. Stephen King.   5. Nana. 6. Charles Dickens. 7. Noddy. 8. A Horse. 9. A Hobbit. 10. Hercule Poirot.*

Literature

AGES 19+

1. Who wrote the horror story 'The Pit and the Pendulum'?

2. Who wrote nonsense verse including the poem 'The Owl and the Pussycat'?

3. Which English romantic poet wrote 'Ode to a Nightingale'?

4. What is the name of the first Harry Potter book?

5. With which satirical magazine is Ian Hislop associated?

6. What was the title of Sir Alex Ferguson's best-selling autobiography?

7. To which famous poet was the author of 'Frankenstein' married?

8. Which prolific author is in 'The Guinness Book of Records' for writing 26 books in one year?

9. Who wrote 'The Cider House Rules' and 'The World According to Garp'?

10. What is the name of the little yellow bird in 'Peanuts'?

Answers: *1. Edgar Allen Poe. 2. Edward Lear. 3. John Keats. 4. Harry Potter and the Philosopher's Stone. 5. Private Eye. 6. Managing My Life. 7. Percy Shelley. 8. Barbara Cartland. 9. John Irving. 10. Woodstock.*

HEROES AND VILLAINS

AGES 12 AND UNDER

1. What is Superman's home planet?

2. At the siege of Troy, who killed Achilles with an arrow?

3. Which Daniel Defoe character spent 24 years marooned on a desert island?

4. What is the home town of Fireman Sam?

5. Who does Dr Banner turn into when he loses his temper?

6. Which employee of Hogwarts School owns a dog called Fang?

7. In which country was Osama Bin Laden born?

8. In which British city did Burke and Hare steal bodies for Doctor Knox?

9. Which Charles Dickens novel features a convict called Mr Magwitch?

10. Traditionally, witches hold their meetings on which night of the week?

Answers: *1. Krypton. 2. Paris. 3. Robinson Crusoe. 4. Pontypandy. 5. The Incredible Hulk. 6. Hagrid. 7. Saudi Arabia. 8. Edinburgh. 9. Great Expectations. 10. Friday.*

Heroes and Villains

Ages 13-18

1. In which month of the year was John F Kennedy assassinated?

2. Who led the Mutiny on The Bounty?

3. In which American city did Al Capone operate?

4. Which leader said, 'Veni, Vidi, Vici'?

5. What is the surname of Harry Potter's evil Uncle Vernon?

6. Who was King of England during World War II?

7. Which cartoon villain vies with Popeye for the attention of Olive Oyl?

8. Which Shakespeare play features the villain, Shylock?

9. Was Leon Trotsky killed with a dagger, an icepick or a revolver?

10. Which building did King Kong carry Fay Wray to the top of?

Answers: *1. November. 2. Fletcher Christian. 3. Chicago. 4. Julius Caesar. 5. Dursley. 6. George VI. 7. Bluto. 8. The Merchant of Venice. 9. An Icepick. 10. The Empire State Building.*

Heroes and Villains

AGES 19+

1. What is the surname of the central family in 'The Godfather' trilogy?

2. Which jockey received a prison sentence for tax evasion in 1987?

3. Who was beheaded for treason at Fotheringay Castle in 1587?

4. Which pink aliens lived on a blue moon with the Soup Dragon and the Froglets?

5. Who played Starsky in the TV series 'Starsky and Hutch'?

6. Who played one third of The Witches of Eastwick and one half of Thelma and Louise?

7. In what year was the Yorkshire Ripper arrested?

8. In World War II, which British singer was nicknamed 'The Forces Sweetheart'?

9. Which Bond villain had three nipples?

10. The name of which Roman Emperor means 'little boots'?

Answers: *1. Corleone.   2. Lester Piggott.   3. Mary Queen of Scots.   4. The Clangers.   5. Paul Michael Glaser.   6. Susan Sarandon.   7. 1981.   8. Vera Lynn.   9. Scaramanga.   10. Caligula.*

SPORT

AGES 12 AND UNDER

1. What is the name given to a kick in Rugby Union, which follows a try?

2. In which sport does the pitcher stand on a mound in the middle of a diamond?

3. In snooker what colour comes next in this sequence: yellow, green, brown, blue,…?

4. In which sport is the winning team required to travel a distance of 3.6 metres?

5. Which British city plays host to football's Old Firm derby?

6. How many points does a canon score in billiards?

7. What do the initials GS stand for on a netball shirt?

8. In which country did the martial art of Tai Chi originate?

9. Which country does Australia play cricket against when competing for the Worrell Trophy?

10. In which sport is the net 15.25 centimetres high?

Answers: *1. A Conversion. 2. Baseball. 3. Pink. 4. Tug of War. 5. Glasgow. 6. Two. 7. Goal Shooter. 8. China. 9. The West Indies. 10. Table Tennis.*

Sport

AGES 13-18

1. In which Olympic event are competitors required to wear a top hat?

2. What sport is played by the Brisbane Lions?

3. Which letter of the Greek alphabet is also the name of a sporting goods manufacturer?

4. What takes place in a ring called a dojo?

5. What bird features on the badge of Tottenham Hotspur football club?

6. Which is the largest: a golf ball, a squash ball or a table tennis ball?

7. Which American city hosts the Indy 500 motor race?

8. At Augusta golf course, all the holes are named after what?

9. Which Scottish football club plays its home matches at Rugby Park?

10. What do the letters LB stand for with regard to a position in American Football?

Answers: 1. Dressage. 2. Australian Rules Football. 3. Kappa. 4. Sumo Wrestling. 5. A Cockerel. 6. A Golf Ball. 7. Indianapolis. 8. Flowers and Plants. 9. Kilmarnock. 10. Linebacker.

Sport

AGES 19+

1. Which European nation hosted the first Winter Olympics?

2. Which British golf course is home to 'The Valley of Sin'?

3. In which city is the Hungarian Grand Prix held?

4. In which sport would you use the term 'southpaw'?

5. What two colours are the bottom two rings on the Olympic flag?

6. At which course is 'The Oaks' horserace held?

7. In which sport is the Jarvis Cup contested?

8. In what year was Nigel Mansell crowned Formula 1 World Champion?

9. From what wood are cricket bats traditionally made?

10. Which country was the host of football's 1978 World Cup?

Answers: *1. France. 2. St. Andrews. 3. Budapest. 4. Boxing. 5. Yellow and Green. 6. Epsom. 7. Squash. 8. 1992. 9. Willow. 10. Argentina.*

SPELLING

AGES 12 AND UNDER

Spell:

1. FACILITY

2. CEILING

3. BURGLAR

4. CALCULATOR

5. EXCEL

6. ACTION

7. SOLDIER

8. FOREIGN

9. EQUIP

10. ATTACH

Spelling

AGES 13-18

Spell:

1. CONCLUSION

2. CONSCIOUS

3. IMAGINARY

4. INTERRUPT

5. DIAMOND

6. KNOWLEDGE

7. BUSINESS

8. PERSUADE

9. PHYSICAL

10. SEQUENCE

<u>Spelling</u>

AGES 19+

Spell:

1. MISCELLANEOUS

2. QUESTIONNAIRE

3. INDEPENDENCE

4. BALLERINA

5. DEFINITELY

6. OCCURRENCE

7. PARALLEL

8. CONNOISSEUR

9. EMBARRASS

10. GRIEVANCE

WORDS

AGES 12 AND UNDER

1. What seven-letter H word is the name for a leather case that holds a pistol or revolver?

2. What is the American equivalent of a Russian Cosmonaut?

3. What does the French word 'bonjour' mean?

4. What word means both 'to invent' and 'cosmetics'?

5. Which K word is another term for tomato sauce?

6. What sort of animal is a pug?

7. What is the past tense of the word 'drink'?

8. What name is given to a fertile place in a desert?

9. What sort of words are run, jump, talk and fall?

10. What is the word 'fridge' short for?

Answers: *1. Holster. 2. Astronaut. 3. Hello (Good Day). 4. Make Up. 5. Ketchup. 6. A Dog. 7. Drank. 8. An Oasis. 9. Verbs. 10. Refrigerator.*

Words

AGES 13-18

1. What name is given to a judge's small wooden hammer?

2. What special feature do words or phrases that are palindromes have?

3. What word do Americans use for the boot of a car?

4. What word is used to describe a group of crows?

5. What book gives lists of words with similar meanings?

6. What word do Americans use for an 'undertaker'?

7. What is a tsunami?

8. Of what is demography the study?

9. What is the second word of the Lord's Prayer?

10. Which chess piece is sometimes called a rook?

Answers: *1. A Gavel. 2. They read the same forwards as they do backwards. 3. Trunk. 4. A Murder. 5. A Thesaurus. 6. A Mortician. 7. A Tidal Wave. 8. Populations. 9. Father. 10. The Castle.*

Words

AGES 19+

1. From whom do these words originally come: 'Don't count your chickens before they are hatched'?

2. What does the acronym WYSIWYG stand for?

3. What is the common name for the patella?

4. What word do we get from Ambrose Everett Burnside, referring to our hair?

5. What colour is angelica?

6. From which language does the word algebra originate?

7. What is the American word for grilling food?

8. What is the more common French name for zucchini?

9. From which language do the words taffeta, bazaar and caravan originate?

10. Whose last words were reportedly: 'Oh, I am so bored with it all'?

Answers: *1. Aesop. 2. What You See Is What You Get. 3. The kneecap. 4. Sideburns. 5. Green. 6. Arabic. 7. Broiling. 8. Courgette. 9. Persian. 10. Winston Churchill.*

THE HUMAN BODY

AGES 12 AND UNDER

1. On which part of the body do cowboys wear chaps?

2. How many lungs does the human body contain?

3. Chiropody is the treatment of which part of your body?

4. Around which part of your body might you wear a 'dicky bow'?

5. What type of body part are triceps?

6. Which part of your body features a cornea?

7. Which substance transports oxygen around the human body?

8. Where in your body would you find metacarpal bones?

9. What is the longest bone in the human body?

10. What is another name for the trachea?

Answers: *1. Legs. 2. Two. 3. Feet. 4. Neck. 5. Muscles. 6. The Eye. 7. Blood. 8. The Hands. 9. The Femur (Thigh Bone). 10. The Windpipe.*

The Human Body

AGES 13-18

1. What is the largest artery travelling from the human heart called?

2. Where in the human body would you find bones called the stirrup and the anvil?

3. How many litres of blood would you find in an adult human body?

4. Where would you find your Achilles tendon?

5. Does food travel through your stomach or large intestine first?

6. Where is your clavicle bone?

7. What is the average human body temperature to the nearest whole number, in centigrade?

8. Which part of the body secretes the hormone insulin?

9. What is the name of the hole in your eye that lets in light?

10. How many pairs of chromosomes does a human being have?

Answers: *1. The Aorta. 2. The Ear. 3. Five Litres. 4. Your Foot (the heel). 5. Stomach. 6. In Your Shoulder. 7. 37 Degrees Centigrade. 8. The Pancreas. 9. The Pupil. 10. 23.*

The Human Body

AGES 19+

1. What does the A stand for in the acronym DNA?

2. Which is the largest organ in the human body?

3. How many bones make up the vertebral column?

4. The palatine glands are more commonly known as what?

5. Which pea-sized gland, which is located in the skull, releases hormones that affect metabolism?

6. How long, to the nearest foot, is the small intestine?

7. In which part of the body would you find papillae?

8. What is the name of the walnut sized gland found only in men?

9. In which part of the body is the occipital bone?

10. What is the technical name for the shoulder blade?

Answers: *1. Acid. 2. The Skin. 3. 33. 4. Tonsils. 5. Pituitary Gland. 6. 10 Feet. 7. The Tongue.*

8. The Prostate. 9. The Head. 10. The Scapula.

ANIMALS

AGES 12 AND UNDER

1. What is a male elephant called?

2. What type of animal is a bustard?

3. What is a Chow?

4. What unusual pet did Julius Caesar own?

5. Is a Sole a freshwater or saltwater fish?

6. Which animal represents the star sign Capricorn?

7. What is a leveret?

8. Who, in the Bible, was swallowed alive by a whale?

9. What creature would you be eating if you were served calamari?

10. Which fish makes spectacular leaps upstream to return to its birthplace?

Answers: *1. A Bull. 2. A Bird. 3. A Breed of Dog. 4. A Giraffe. 5. Saltwater. 6. A Goat. 7. A Young Hare. 8. Jonah. 9. Squid. 10. The Salmon.*

Animals

Ages 13-18

1. What are the horns of a stag called?

2. What sort of animal was Tarka?

3. What collective noun is used for a group of kangaroos?

4. How many toes does an ostrich have on each foot?

5. Which country has more cattle than any other?

6. What bird is the symbol of the French Rugby Team?

7. Gorillas are found in how many continents?

8. Which is the longest living animal?

9. What kind of creature is an ocelot?

10. Which insect carries the disease malaria?

Answers: *1. Antlers. 2. An Otter. 3. A Troop. 4. Two. 5. India. 6. A Cockerel. 7. One (Africa). 8. The Giant Tortoise. 9. A Cat. 10. The Mosquito.*

Animals

AGES 19+

1. Which is larger: the alligator or the crocodile?

2. In which continent would you find the snow leopard?

3. How many legs does a lobster have?

4. Which creature has the largest eye in the animal kingdom?

5. Which is the fastest: a black mamba snake, a chicken or a pig?

6. What is a peccary?

7. In which river do you find the world's largest crocodiles?

8. How many stomachs does a camel have?

9. Which two animals are crossed to create a mule?

10. In which century did the Dodo become extinct?

Answers: *1. Crocodile. 2. Asia. 3. Ten. 4. The Giant Squid. 5. A Black Mamba Snake. 6. A Wild Pig. 7. The Nile. 8. Four. 9. A Horse and A Donkey. 10. 17th Century.*

PEOPLE

AGES 12 AND UNDER

1. By what title is the Bishop of Rome also known?

2. Which planet did William Herschel discover in 1781?

3. Which European country did Benito Mussolini rule during World War II?

4. Which famous explorer died penniless in 1506?

5. Which American President was assassinated in 1963?

6. Which country did Cleopatra rule?

7. How did Joan of Arc die?

8. What sport does Prince Charles play on horseback using a mallet?

9. Lord Baden Powell founded which movement?

10. What was the first name of the composer Beethoven?

Answers: *1. The Pope. 2. Uranus. 3. Italy. 4. Christopher Columbus. 5. John F Kennedy. 6. (Ancient) Egypt. 7. Burned at the Stake. 8. Polo. 9. The Scouts. 10. Ludwig.*

People

AGES 13-18

1. How many English kings have been called Edward?

2. Which Greek philosopher was made to commit suicide by drinking Hemlock?

3. What nationality was the composer Richard Wagner?

4. What sort of stories are associated with the writer Hans Christian Andersen?

5. Which Yuri was the first person in Space?

6. American singer Stefani Joanne Angelina Germanotta is best known by which stage name?

7. Which island nation is pop star Rihanna from?

8. Tom Cruise is an outspoken member of which religion?

9. What is the surname of the Italian fashion designer Donatella?

10. What was aviation pioneer Lindbergh's first name?

Answers: *1. Eight. 2. Socrates. 3. German. 4. Fairytales. 5. Yuri Gagarin. 6. Lady Gaga. 7. Barbados. 8. Scientology. 9. Versace. 10. Charles.*

People

AGES 19+

1. In what decade of the twentieth century was the actress Goldie Hawn born?

2. Mark Spitz won seven Olympic golds – in which city?

3. Carrie Fisher is which actress' daughter?

4. What politician referred to 'drawing a line in the sand' regarding the Gulf War?

5. Who succeeded Mikhail Gorbachev as Russian leader?

6. Whose marriage was headlined in Variety magazine as 'Egghead weds Hourglass'?

7. Chevy Chase was a professional in which sport?

8. Who did Stella McCartney replace as designer at Chloe?

9. In which decade did Andy Warhol die?

10. What is the stage name of Stevland Hardaway Judkins?

Answers: *1. 1940s. 2. Munich. 3. Debbie Reynolds. 4. George Bush (Snr.). 5. Boris Yeltsin. 6. Arthur Miller and Marilyn Monroe. 7. Tennis. 8. Karl Lagerfeld. 9. 1980s. 10. Stevie Wonder.*

SCIENCE

AGES 12 AND UNDER

1. Are all metals magnetic?

2. What is the chemical symbol for Chlorine?

3. Is the Sun a hundred, a thousand or a million times bigger than Earth?

4. Who wrote 'A Brief History of Time'?

5. What does a barometer measure?

6. What is the name of the Spaceman in Toy Story 2?

7. Hydroponics is the science of growing plants without what usual component?

8. Are mammals warm or cold blooded?

9. Which part of a plant takes in water?

10. Is the male part of a flower called the stigma, the petal or the stamen?

Answers: 1. No. 2. Cl. 3. A Million. 4. Stephen Hawking. 5. Atmospheric Pressure. 6. Buzz Lightyear. 7. Soil. 8. Warm blooded. 9. The Roots. 10. Stamen.

Science

AGES 13-18

1. What does an invertebrate not have?

2. What is the chemical symbol for Iron?

3. What substance makes leaves green?

4. Who wrote 'On the Origin of Species'?

5. What does a seismograph measure?

6. Who made over 1,000 inventions, including the phonograph and practical electric lighting?

7. Hydroponics is the science of growing plants without what usual component?

8. Carbohydrates contain three elements: carbon, hydrogen and which other?

9. Which is the second largest planet in our solar system?

10. In physics, what is the name given to a rod that turns around a fixed point?

Answers: *1. A Backbone. 2. Fe. 3. Chlorophyll. 4. Charles Darwin. 5. Earthquakes. 6. Thomas Edison. 7. Soil. 8. Oxygen. 9. Saturn. 10. A Lever.*

Science

AGES 19+

1. How many bones are found in the human body?

2. What is the chemical symbol for Manganese?

3. What is the most abundant gas in the Earth's atmosphere?

4. What is the hardest natural substance on Earth?

5. Which oath of ethics is taken by doctors?

6. What was the name of the first man-made satellite launched by the Soviet Union in 1957?

7. What is the lightest metal?

8. Who discovered radio waves?

9. Out of the seven colours of the rainbow, which one lies in the middle?

10. For what do the initials USB stand?

Answers: *1. 206. 2. Mn. 3. Nitrogen. 4. Diamond. 5. Hippocratic Oaths. 6. Sputnik 1. 7. Lithium. 8. (Heinrich) Hertz. 9. Green. 10. Universal Serial Bus.*

NUMBERS

AGES 12 AND UNDER

1. How many cents in an American quarter?

2. How many days in a leap year?

3. How many letters in the alphabet?

4. What is the square root of 121?

5. How many 10p pieces are there in £20?

6. How many hours are there in 3 days?

7. How many eighths are there in one half?

8. How many threes are there in 102?

9. In Roman numerals what number is represented by XIV?

10. How many sides does a quadrilateral have?

Answers: *1. 25   2. 36   3. 26   4. 11   5. 200   6. 72   7. 4   8. 34   9. 14   10. 4*

Numbers

AGES 12 AND UNDER

1. How many cents in an American dime?

2. How many days in ten years, including two leap years?

3. How many letters in the Greek alphabet?

4. What is the square root of 144?

5. How many 10p pieces are there in £20.40?

6. How many hours are there in 7 days?

7. How many eighths are there in one quarter?

8. How many sixes are there in 102?

9. In Roman numerals what number is represented by XIX?

10. How many sides does a nonagon have?

Answers: *1. 10   2. 3652   3. 24   4. 12   5. 204   6. 168   7. 2   8. 17   9. 19   10. 9*

<u>Numbers</u>

Ages 19+

1. How many cents in an American nickel?

2. How many days in 45 weeks?

3. How many letters in the Russian alphabet?

4. What is the square root of 324?

5. How many 5p pieces are there in £20.40?

6. How many minutes are there in 1 day?

7. How many eighths are there in three quarters?

8. How many sixes are there in 204?

9. In Roman numerals what number is represented by CXXXVII?

10. How many faces does a dodecahedron have?

Answers: *1. 10   2. 315   3. 32   4. 12   5. 408   6. 1440   7. 6   8. 34   9. 137   10. 12*

FOOD & DRINK

AGES 12 AND UNDER

1. From which country does spaghetti originate?

2. Which part of the coffee plant is harvested to make the drink?

3. What is Brie an example of?

4. Which tree gives its name to the syrup you pour over pancakes?

5. From which vegetable is sauerkraut made?

6. Which substance makes bread rise?

7. What is mulligatawny?

8. What is the main ingredient of an omelette?

9. Which vegetable was turned into a carriage in Cinderella?

10. Which drink is also the name given to the left side of a ship?

Answers: 1. Italy. 2. The Beans. 3. Cheese. 4. Maple. 5. Cabbage. 6. Yeast. 7. A Soup. 8. Eggs. 9. A Pumpkin. 10. Port.

Food & Drink

AGES 13-18

1. What flavour is the drink crème de menthe?

2. In which decade of the 20th century were tea bags invented?

3. From which country does the wine Liebfraumilch come?

4. From which country do we get the rice dish risotto?

5. What is the main vegetable ingredient of the Russian soup, borscht?

6. What is Popeye's favourite food?

7. Which part of a rhubarb plant is poisonous?

8. What other name is often given to the aubergine?

9. From which fish do we get caviar?

10. What kind of animal is a halibut?

Answers: *1. Mint. 2. 1920s. 3. Germany. 4. Italy. 5. Beetroot. 6. Spinach. 7. Its leaves. 8. Eggplant. 9. The Sturgeon. 10. A Fish.*

Food & Drink

Ages 19+

1. Lady Finger is a variety of which fruit?

2. Which vitamin are mushrooms high in?

3. Which nut do you find in pesto?

4. What does IPA stand for?

5. From which country do Granny Smith apples originate?

6. Which country produces the most potatoes?

7. Which fruit has varieties including Tommy Atkins, Kent and Francis?

8. What type of pastry are profiteroles made from?

9. Chives are a member of which family of vegetable?

10. Which pungent plant has its own festival held on the Isle of Wight every year?

Answers: *1. Banana. 2. Vitamin B. 3. Pine Nuts. 4. Indian Pale Ale. 5. Australia. 6. China. 7. Mango. 8. Choux. 9. Onion. 10. Garlic.*

ART

AGES 12 AND UNDER

1. What colour do you get if you mix yellow and blue?

2. Who painted The Mona Lisa?

3. Works of art, which are not life-like or realistic, are sometimes referred to as what?

4. Salvatore Ferragamo famously designed which item of clothing?

5. Andy Goldsworthy is noted for his sculptures made from what?

6. What is the name given to the flat board on which an artist lays and mixes paint colours?

7. Who painted 'The Scream'?

8. What are the three primary colours?

9. How long did Leonardo Da Vinci spend painting the Mona Lisa's lips: 12 days, 12 weeks or 12 years?

10. In which country was the first pencil invented?

Answers: *1. Green. 2. Leonardo Da Vinci. 3. Abstract. 4. Shoes. 5. Naturally found materials (leaves, twigs, flowers etc.). 6. A Palette. 7. Munch. 8. Red, Yellow and Blue. 9. 12 years. 10. England (in the 1500s).*

Art

AGES 13-18

1. What famous 20th Century American artist painted the Pop Art piece, '100 Cans'?

2. Who painted 'Guernica'?

3. In which city would you find The Louvre art museum?

4. Who designed the Guggenheim Museum?

5. Which French artist is most famous for his obsession with ballerinas?

6. In which Italian town was Leonardo Da Vinci born?

7. Which painter cut off a part of his ear?

8. Black and white are not colours. What are they?

9. What is unusual about the Mona Lisa's face in Da Vinci's painting?

10. Which historical period has a French name that translates to 'rebirth' in English?

Answers: *1. Andy Warhol. 2. Pablo Picasso. 3. Paris. 4. Frank Lloyd Wright. 5. (Edgar) Degas. 6. Vinci. 7. Vincent Van Gogh. 8. Shades. 9. She Has No Eyebrows. 10. The Renaissance.*

Art

AGES 19+

1. Which American abstract expressionist was known for using the 'drip technique'?

2. Name the extravagant period of art and architecture prevalent in Europe in the 17th Century?

3. Salvador Dali is associated with which art movement?

4. Who painted 'Girl Before a Mirror' and 'The Weeping Woman'?

5. Vincent Van Gogh had an older brother who died at birth. What was his name?

6. What is the true art name for colour?

7. Pablo Picasso's full name contains how many words: 3, 13 or 23?

8. Botticelli's 'Birth of Venus' features a goddess floating in the ocean on what?

9. In which country was Pablo Picasso born?

10. What year was Pablo Picasso born?

Answers: *1. Jackson Pollock. 2. The Baroque Period. 3. Surrealism. 4. Pablo Picasso. 5. Vincent. 6. Hue. 7. 23. 8. A Seashell. 9. Spain. 10. 1881 (give a point for any answer between 1875 and 1890).*

PASTIMES & HOBBIES

AGES 12 AND UNDER

1. What is the points' value of the letter E in Scrabble?

2. How many red balls are on the table at the beginning of a frame of snooker?

3. What is the highest score that can be made by a single dart on a dartboard?

4. What do Numismatists collect?

5. What is the name of the small white ball in Bowls?

6. What is the largest freshwater fish you can catch in the UK?

7. In Bingo, which number is referred to as 'two fat ladies'?

8. Which martial art translates as 'way of the empty hand'?

9. In which month does grouse shooting season commence?

10. Earth is 93 million miles from which star?

Answers: 1. 1. 2. 15. 3. 60. 4. Coins (or medals). 5. The Jack. 6. Pike. 7. 88. 8. Karate. 9. August. 10. The Sun.

Pastimes & Hobbies

AGES 13-18

1. What is the points' value of the letter K in Scrabble?

2. What total is the 'maximum' break in snooker?

3. What is the lowest score that can be made by a single dart on a dartboard?

4. What do Philatelists collect?

5. What is a Neon Tetra?

6. What is the common name for the garden plant digitalis?

7. In Bingo, which number is referred to as 'two little ducks'?

8. Which martial art translates as 'gentle way'?

9. In which month does salmon fishing commence in Scotland?

10. How many Zodiac Constellations are there?

Answers: 1. 5. 2. 147. 3. 23. 4. Postage Stamps. 5. A Tropical Fish. 6. Foxglove. 7. 22. 8. Judo. 9. February. 10. 12.

Pastimes & Hobbies

AGES 19+

1. What is the points' value of the letter J in Scrabble?

2. What is the value of the green ball in snooker?

3. What is the fewest number of darts you would need to throw for the perfect score of 501?

4. What are Ferroequinologists interested in?

5. What playing card is referred to as the Black Lady?

6. In Bridge, what jargon word is used to describe the condition of holding no trumps?

7. In Bingo, which number is referred to as 'doctor's orders'?

8. How many playing pieces are there in a set of dominoes?

9. Court cards on British playing cards are costumed from the time of which monarch?

10. What is the highest hand in Poker?

Answers: *1. 8. 2. 15. 3. 9. 4. Trains (Rail Transport). 5. The Queen of Spades. 6. Chicane. 7. 9. 8. 36. 9. Henry VII or Henry VIII (accept either answer). 10. A Royal Flush.*

WARS

AGES 12 AND UNDER

1. Which country joined World War I in April 1917?

2. What is a blunderbuss?

3. Who was Emperor of Japan during World War II?

4. In which decade was the Korean War fought?

5. In the Trojan Wars, which side used a wooden horse to enter the city of Troy?

6. Germany and Japan were two of the main Axis powers in World War II; name one other.

7. Which two countries fought the Battle of Agincourt?

8. What was the name of the German air force in World War II?

9. Which Asian war took place between 1965 and 1973?

10. Which famous English army leader was known as the Iron Duke?

Answers: *1. The United States of America. 2. A Type of Gun. 3. Hirohito. 4. The 1950s. 5. The Greeks. 6. Italy, Bulgaria or Romania. 7. France and England. 8. The Luftwaffe. 9. The Vietnam War. 10. The Duke of Wellington.*

Wars

AGES 13-18

1. Was General Patton British, German, American or Italian?

2. At the end of which war was the United Nations formed?

3. Which South American country did Pizarro conquer in 1533?

4. Who was President of the USA during World War I?

5. Who was 'Monty' of the Desert Rats?

6. Which two royal houses fought the War of the Roses?

7. In the English Civil War, what name was given to the anti-royalists?

8. What does the 'VJ' stand for in VJ Day?

9. In what year did Japan bomb Pearl Harbor?

10. What name was given to the South's forces in the American Civil War?

Answers: *1. American. 2. World War II. 3. Peru. 4. Woodrow Wilson. 5. Field Marshall Montgomery. 6. York and Lancaster. 7. The Roundheads. 8. Victory in Japan. 9. 1941. 10. The Confederates.*

Wars

AGES 19+

1. Whose forces were defeated at the Battle of Actium?

2. In 1979, which country was invaded by Soviet troops?

3. Name one of the two States that the U.S. and Mexico fought over between 1846 and 1848?

4. Who was the last British King to die in battle?

5. What deadly gas was first used at the Battle of Ypres in 1915?

6. Which revolt did Wat Tyler lead in 1381?

7. Which German ship was sunk at the Battle of the River Plate?

8. Which general led the North's forces in the American Civil War?

9. Who led the Afrika Korps in World War II?

10. In which century did the French Revolution occur?

Answers: *1. Cleopatra and Mark Antony. 2. Afghanistan. 3. Texas & California. 4. Richard III. 5. Chlorine. 6. The Peasants' Revolt. 7. Graf Spee. 8. Ulysses S. Grant. 9. General Rommel. 10. The 18th Century.*

CELEBRITIES

AGES 12 AND UNDER

1. Which arch-enemy of Peter Pan was played by Dustin Hoffman on film?

2. Live Aid was a charity concert in aid of which famine-stricken African country?

3. Which popular duo present Britain's Got Talent?

4. What nationality is the actor Jude Law?

5. In which soap is the local newspaper called the Walford Gazette?

6. Who wrote the music for 'The Lion King'?

7. Which band was nicknamed The Fab Four?

8. Of which band was Harry Styles a member?

9. How many bathrooms does Bill Gates' house have: 4, 14, 24 or 34?

10. Which Australian actress was once married to Tom Cruise?

Answers: *1. Captain Hook. 2. Ethiopia. 3. Ant and Dec. 4. British. 5. EastEnders. 6. Elton John. 7. The Beatles. 8. One Direction. 9. 24. 10. Nicole Kidman.*

Celebrities

AGES 13-18

1. Which American tennis star was nicknamed Superbrat?

2. What is Taylor Swift's middle name?

3. Who won the Brit Award for Best Female Solo Artist in 2020?

4. What nationality is the actor Will Ferrell?

5. What is the pub on Coronation Street called?

6. What is the real name of the actor known as 'The Rock'?

7. In which city did Ant and Dec grow up?

8. Which famous couple's children are called Rumi and Sir?

9. Which singer has guitars called Felix and Sally?

10. Which James Bond theme song did Adele top the charts with in 2012?

Answers: *1. John McEnroe. 2. Alison. 3. Mabel. 4. American. 5. The Rovers Return (Inn). 6. Dwayne Johnson. 7. Newcastle (upon-Tyne). 8. Beyoncé and Jay-Z. 9. Ed Sheeran. 10. Skyfall.*

Celebrities

AGES 19+

1. What is Sporty Spice, Mel C's, real name?

2. Which Australian soap started the career of Kylie Minogue?

3. In which Oscar winning film was Mia Farrow married to Michael Caine?

4. To which actress is Peter Sarsgaard married?

5. What is the stage name of drummer Richard Starkey?

6. In which band was Michael Hutchence the lead singer?

7. In which U.S. town was the comedy 'Cheers' set?

8. Who was Blur's lead singer?

9. Which actor recorded an album called Willennium?

10. Name Angelina Jolie's actor father.

Answers: *1. Melanie Chisholm. 2. Neighbours. 3. Hannah and her Sisters. 4. Maggie Gyllenhaal. 5. Ringo Starr. 6. INXS. 7. Boston. 8. Damon Albarn. 9. Will Smith. 10. Jon Voight.*

RELIGION

AGES 12 AND UNDER

1. Which religion was introduced into Japan in the 6th Century?

2. Which religion is influenced by the prophet Muhammad?

3. Which scrolls were discovered in Jordan in 1947?

4. Which Indian leader was known as The Mahatma, meaning 'great soul'?

5. Which historic city is considered a holy place by Christians, Jews and Muslims?

6. Who lives in a monastery?

7. Who sentenced Jesus to death?

8. Who is the patron saint of travellers?

9. In which year were the Dead Sea Scrolls discovered? (Do not repeat Q.3!)

10. Who, according to the Bible, was the oldest man who ever lived?

Answers: *1. Buddhism. 2. Islam. 3. The Dead Sea Scrolls. 4. Gandhi. 5. Jerusalem. 6. Monks. 7. Pontius Pilate. 8. St. Christopher. 9. 1947. 10. Methuselah.*

Religion

AGES 13-18

1. Is Ezra a book of the Old Testament or New Testament?

2. In the Bible, what are the first three words of Genesis?

3. Which Sanskrit words means 'awakened one'?

4. In which country is Islam's holiest city located?

5. Which African country is regarded as the spiritual home of the Rastafari religious movement?

6. What is the last day of Christmas called?

7. In Jewish, Christian and Muslim belief, who led the Hebrew slaves out of Egypt?

8. Who is the Hindu god associated with rain?

9. What is the sacred text of Islam?

10. What festival is associated with the goddess Lakshmi and is a time for lighting festive lamps?

Answers: *1. Old Testament. 2. In the Beginning. 3. Buddha. 4. Saudi Arabia. 5. Ethiopia. 6. Epiphany. 7. Moses. 8. Indra. 9. The Qur'an. 10. Diwali.*

Religion

AGES 19+

1. Which religious leader's teaching consisted of four 'Noble Truths'?

2. Taoism is an ancient religion that originated in which country?

3. What word describes the yearly Islamic pilgrimage to Mecca?

4. Which is the holiest book of Judaism?

5. As of 2021, who is the Archbishop of Canterbury?

6. Which is the largest religion in the world, in terms of the number of believers?

7. Which saint is believed to have introduced Christianity in India?

8. In which religion do men take the last name 'Singh'?

9. What is the name of the Vatican's army?

10. Which book of the Bible comes after Acts?

Answers: 1. Buddha. 2. China. 3. Hajj. 4. The Torah. 5. Justin Welby. 6. Christianity. 7. St. Thomas. 8. Sikhism. 9. The Swiss Guard. 10. Romans.

TRANSPORT

AGES 12 AND UNDER

1. What type of boat is steered by a gondolier?

2. Which form of transport has gears, forks, a chainstay and pedals?

3. What colour are taxis in New York?

4. Which was the fastest passenger-carrying aeroplane ever made?

5. Which carmaker's previous models include the Capri and the Anglia?

6. What colour was the Beatles' submarine?

7. How old do you have to be to hold a full driving licence in Britain?

8. What is the meaning of the initials UFO?

9. Which transport system features the Piccadilly and Bakerloo lines?

10. What is Russia's national airline called?

Answers: *1. Gondola. 2. A Bicycle. 3. Yellow. 4. Concorde. 5. Ford. 6. Yellow. 7. 17. 8. Unidentified Flying Object. 9. The London Underground. 10. Aeroflot.*

Transport

AGES 13-18

1. What is Europe's busiest airport?

2. Which two English cities does the Grand Union Canal link?

3. What is the national airline of Spain?

4. Which canal connects the Mediterranean Sea to the Red Sea?

5. With what sort of transport is the term 'stealth' associated?

6. What form of transport was the Hindenberg an example?

7. George Stephenson invented what form of transport?

8. What sort of vehicle did Sir Christopher Cockerell invent?

9. What is the name of the rod on a car that joins two wheels together?

10. What is Australia's national airline called?

Answers: *1. Heathrow. 2. Liverpool and Manchester. 3. Iberia. 4. The Suez Canal. 5. (Military) Aircraft. 6. (Passenger) Airship. 7. The Steam Locomotive. 8. The Hovercraft. 9. The Axle. 10. QANTAS.*

Transport

Ages 19+

1. The first passenger railway opened in 1825 between two English towns: name one of them.

2. Who invented the first car driven by an internal combustion engine?

3. Which London Underground line is coloured red on the map?

4. On which continent are Airbus aircraft manufactured?

5. Which name is given to the American intercity bus carrier, which began life in Minnesota in 1914?

6. Which taxi service in Bangkok gets its name from the sputtering sound of its engine?

7. O'Hare International Airport is located in which American city?

8. Volvo cars are from which country?

9. The original Orient Express ran between Venice and which other city?

10. What is Indonesia's national airline called?

Answers: *1. Stockton and Darlington. 2. (Karl) Benz. 3. Central Line. 4. Europe. 5. Greyhound. 6. Tuk Tuk. 7. Chicago. 8. Sweden. 9. Istanbul. 10. Garuda.*

SINGLE LETTER ANSWER

AGES 12 AND UNDER

1. Which letter denotes the Roman numeral for one hundred?

2. Desmond Llewelyn was known for playing which role in James Bond movies?

3. Which letter has a value of 5 points in Scrabble?

4. What is Homer Simpson's middle name initial?

5. Which vitamin is required to prevent rickets?

6. What is the only letter that does not appear in the name of any US State?

7. Which letter is the most commonly used in the English alphabet?

8. What is the chemical symbol for Carbon?

9. Which single letter follows Elizabeth when the Queen signs her name?

10. Which letter is to the right of the letter Q on the top row of a keyboard?

Answers: *1. C. 2. Q. 3. K. 4. J. 5. D. 6. Q. 7. E. 8. C. 9. R. 10. W.*

Single Letter Answer

AGES 13-18

1. Which letter denotes the Roman numeral for fifty?

2. Judi Dench was known for playing which role in James Bond movies?

3. Name one of the two letters that has a value of 8 points in Scrabble.

4. What is Joanne Rowling's middle name initial?

5. Which vitamin is required to prevent scurvy?

6. Most worldwide capital cities begin with which letter?

7. Which letter is the second most commonly used in the English alphabet?

8. What is the chemical symbol for Potassium?

9. Which letter is the most recent addition (in 1524) to the English alphabet?

10. Which letter is to the right of the letter S on the middle row of a keyboard?

Answers: 1. L. 2. M. 3. J or X. 4. K. 5. C. 6. B. 7. A. 8. K. 9. J. 10. D.

Single Letter Answer

AGES 19+

1. Which letter denotes the Roman numeral for five hundred?

2. How was Welsh singer Ian Watkins known professionally?

3. Name one of the two letters that has a value of 10 points in Scrabble.

4. What is Samuel Jackson's middle name initial?

5. Which vitamin is required to prevent 'night blindness'?

6. In Morse Code, what letter is represented by three dashes?

7. Which letter is the third most commonly used in the English alphabet?

8. What is the chemical symbol for Tungsten?

9. Which is the only letter in the English alphabet that is never silent?

10. Which letter is to the right of the letter V on the bottom row of a keyboard?

Answers: *1. D. 2. H. 3. Q or Z. 4. L. 5. A. 6. O. 7. R. 8. W. 9. V. 10. B.*

TRUE OR FALSE?

AGES 12 AND UNDER

1. Prince Harry is taller than Prince William.

2. The unicorn is the national animal of Scotland.

3. A lion's roar can be heard up to 8 kilometres away.

4. Australia is wider than the moon.

5. An octopus has three hearts.

6. Harry Styles' middle name is Edward.

7. In 'Harry Potter', Draco Malfoy has no siblings.

8. A cara cara navel is a type of orange.

9. Monaco is the smallest country in the world.

10. The letter X is worth 10 points in Scrabble.

Answers: *1. False. 2. True. 3. True. 4. True. 5. True. 6. True. 7. False. 8. True. 9. False. 10. False.*

True or False?

AGES 13-18

1. Marrakesh is the capital of Morocco.

2. Waterloo has the greatest number of tube platforms in London.

3. M&M stands for Mars and Moordale.

4. The Great Wall of China is longer than the distance between London and Beijing.

5. Louis Walsh is older than Simon Cowell.

6. Alaska is the biggest American State in square miles.

7. Spaghetto is the singular word for a piece of spaghetti.

8. Cardi B's real name is Cardigan Black.

9. Cinderella was the first Disney princess.

10. There are five different blood groups.

Answers: *1. False. 2. True. 3. False. 4. True. 5. True. 6. True. 7. True. 8. False. 9. False. 10. False.*

True or False?

AGES 19+

1. Meryl Streep has won three Academy Awards (as of 2020).

2. Gin is typically included in a Long Island Iced Tea.

3. Hillary Clinton and Celine Dion are related.

4. There are 196 episodes of Friends.

5. Canis Lupus is the scientific name for a wolf.

6. H&M stands for Hennes and Mauritz.

7. ASOS stands for 'As Seen On Screen'.

8. 'What Do You Mean' was Justin Bieber's first UK Number One.

9. The river Seine in Paris is longer than the river Thames in London.

10. Strictly Come Dancing first aired in the UK in 2005.

Answers: *1. True. 2. True. 3. False. 4. False. 5. True. 6. True. 7. True. 8. True. 9. True. 10. False.*

Printed in Great Britain
by Amazon